African Americans in Sports

Lucent Library of Black History

Other titles in this series:

African Americans in Sports

Lucent Library of Black History

Carla Mooney

LUCENT BOOKS

A part of Gale, Cengage Learning

Detroit • New York • San Francisco • New Haven, Conn • Waterville, Maine • London

LIBRARY OF CONGRESS CATALOGING-IN-PUBLICATION DATA

Mooney, Carla, 1970-
  African Americans in sports / Carla Mooney.
    p. cm. -- (Lucent library of Black history)
  Summary: "The Lucent Library of Black History places important topics (both broad movements as well as more narrowly defined events) in context so that readers will understand the connection between black history and the broad sweep of America's story"-- Provided by publisher.
  Includes bibliographical references and index.
  ISBN 978-1-4205-0675-4 (hardback)
  1. African American athletes--History. 2. Sports--United States--History. 3. Discrimination in sports--United States--History. 4. African American athletes--Social conditions. I. Title.
  GV583.M66 2012
  796.08996073--dc23
                                                          2011035431

Lucent Books
27500 Drake Rd.
Farmington Hills, MI 48331

ISBN-13: 978-1-4205-0675-4
ISBN-10: 1-4205-0675-7

Printed in the United States of America
1 2 3 4 5 6 7 15 14 13 12 11

Contents

Foreword

It has been more than 500 years since Africans were first brought to the New World in shackles, and over 140 years since slavery was formally abolished in the United States. Over 50 years have passed since the fallacy of "separate but equal" was obliterated in the American courts, and some 40 years since the watershed Civil Rights Act of 1965 guaranteed the rights and liberties of all Americans, especially those of color. Over time, these changes have become celebrated landmarks in American history. In the twenty-first century, African American men and women are politicians, judges, diplomats, professors, deans, doctors, artists, athletes, business owners, and home owners. For many, the scars of the past have melted away in the opportunities that have been found in contemporary society. Observers such as Peter N. Kirsanow, who sits on the U.S. Commission of Civil Rights, point to these accomplishments and conclude, "The growing black middle class may be viewed as proof that most of the civil rights battles have been won."

In spite of these legal victories, however, prejudice and inequality have persisted in American society. In 2003, African Americans comprised just 12 percent of the nation's population, yet accounted for 44 percent of its prison inmates and 24 percent of its poor. Racially motivated hate crimes continue to appear on the pages of major newspapers in many American cities. Furthermore, many African Americans still experience either overt or muted racism in their daily lives. A 1996 study undertaken by Professor Nancy Krieger of the Harvard School of Public Health, for example, found that 80 percent of the African American participants reported having experienced racial discrimination in one or more settings, including at work or school, applying for housing and medical care, from the police or in the courts, and on the street or in a public setting.

It is for these reasons that many believe the struggle for racial equality and justice is far from over. These episodes of discrimination threaten to shatter the illusion that America has completely overcome its racist past, causing many black Americans to become increasingly frustrated and confused. Scholar and writer Ellis Cose has described this splintered state in the following way: "I have done everything I was supposed to do. I have stayed out of trouble with the law, gone to the right schools, and worked myself nearly to death. What more do they want? Why in God's name won't they accept me as a full human being?" For Cose and others, the struggle for equality and justice has yet to be fully achieved.

In many subtle yet important ways the traumatic experiences of slavery and segregation continue to inform the way race is discussed and experienced in the twenty-first century. Indeed, it is possible that America will always grapple with the fallout from its distressing past. Ulric Haynes, dean of the Hofstra University School of Business has said, "Perhaps race will always matter, given the historical circumstances under which we came to this country." But studying this past and understanding how it contributes to present-day dialogues about race and history in America is a critical component of contemporary education. To this end, the Lucent Library of Black History offers a thorough look at the experiences that have shaped the black community and the American people as a whole. Annotated bibliographies provide readers with ideas for further research, while fully documented primary and secondary source quotations enhance the text. Each book in the series explores a different episode of black history; together they provide students with a wealth of information as well as launching points for further study and discussion.

African American Trailblazers

When Tony Dungy stepped onto the field for Super Bowl XLI in February 2007, he made history before the first play. As the head coach of the National Football League (NFL) Indianapolis Colts, Dungy and the opposing team's coach, Lovie Smith of the Chicago Bears, became the first African American head coaches in the National Football League's biggest game. A few hours later Dungy made history again when his Colts defeated the Bears 29–17. "I'm proud to be the first African-American coach to win this,"[1] Dungy said during the trophy ceremony.

Not long ago it would have been impossible for many to imagine a black man leading a Super Bowl championship team. Yet on one of sport's biggest stages, Dungy and Smith proved that excellence comes in many colors. In the biggest game of their careers, the men became trailblazers for those who will come after them, just as many African Americans broke through barriers before them. "It is important for me to let people know how proud I am to be here," Dungy said. "It's important for me to let people know [about] the guys who have gone before me, who spurred me on and were my role models."[2]

In the late nineteenth and early twentieth centuries, African American athletes had few opportunities to play. They were banned from most professional sports, following the country's trend of segregation. According to African American tennis star Arthur Ashe:

> In 1888 major-league baseball barred blacks from their teams. Black cyclists were literally run out of the velodromes [bike racing arenas]. College football teams had quotas for blacks. Black tennis players were not accepted on the grass courts of Newport, R.I. The 1920s have been called the Golden Decade of Sports because of the prevalence of such stars as Babe Ruth, Red Grange, Jack Dempsey, Bobby Jones and Bill Tilden. It would be more appropriate to call it the Golden Decade of White Sports, because black athletes were shut out.[3]

Instead of sitting on the sidelines, however, black athletes responded by forming their own clubs, teams, leagues, and tournaments. The Negro National League rose to prominence in baseball. Talented ballplayers entertained thousands of fans. The United Golf Association encouraged African Americans on the greens. In addition, two of the greatest basketball teams in history, the New York Renaissance and the Harlem Globetrotters, grew during the sporting world's segregation.

Baseball player Jackie Robinson is known for breaking the color barrier in baseball. Many remember his accomplishment as one of the most defining moments for African Americans in professional sports. However, lesser-known athletes in a variety of sports also acted as pioneers for their race. Men and women like tennis star Althea Gibson, golfer Charlie Sifford, and track-and-field great Jesse Owens had to be faster, stronger, and more skilled on the field. At the same time, they bore the burden of acting as ambassadors for their race in society.

As they pursued excellence, African American athletes often endured discrimination, insults, and sometimes physical violence. Yet determination to be the best and persistence propelled these men and women. "The black athlete has encountered the ills of a sick society for so long that their determination is far greater than any white athlete,"[4] said Mal Whitfield, a track and field Olympian. For the African American community, black athletes' performances symbolized the hope that they were good enough to share in full citizenship and receive equal treatment.

Indianapolis Colts head coach Tony Dungy, left, meets Chicago Bears head coach Lovie Smith after Super Bowl XLI. It was the first Super Bowl in which both teams were led by African American head coaches. Dungy became the first African American coach to lead his team to a National Football League championship.

Over the years, sports have played a major role in how white America has come to view and accept African Americans. Some African American athletes like basketball great Bill Russell, football star Jim Brown, and world heavyweight champion Muhammad Ali recognized the unique opportunity that came with their athletic accomplishments. Although their stands may not have been popular with mainstream America, these athletes used their sport as a stage to call for equality and highlight the injustice of prejudice. Without the trailblazing men and women of the past, the opportunities for today's African American athletes would not exist. Their sacrifices laid the foundation on which today's superstar athletes like basketball's LeBron James and football's Adrian Peterson stand.

Chapter One

African Americans in Nineteenth-Century Sports

Sports have been part of African Americans' lives for generations. In Africa people raced on foot, in boats, or by swimming. In nineteenth-century America, African American athletes played on baseball teams, played golf and tennis, boxed, and rode horses at racetracks around the country. Most of the time they competed against other black athletes. Sometimes they also competed against white athletes. Although sports began as a form of entertainment, they also became a way for black athletes to escape poverty.

Sports on the Plantation

In the early to mid-nineteenth century, slaves on southern plantations played sports. According to historian David Wiggins, "It was common for planters to pit individual slaves against each other in wrestling and boxing matches. They frequently took place after corn shucking, log rolling, or other communal gatherings when slaves from all over gathered at one particular plantation. Slaveholders liked nothing better than placing a wager or two on their favorite combatant."[5]

Being a good athlete brought a slave prestige and privileges. Victorious athletes earned the respect of fellow slaves. They also became role models for slave children. At the same time, owners valued slave athletes and took pride in their success. As a reward for winning, slave athletes earned privileges that other slaves did not enjoy. They might be allowed a visit to another plantation or an extra ration of food, for instance.

War Brings Change

In 1861 tensions were high between northern and southern states. They argued over trade and slavery. Many people in the North thought slavery should be abolished. When Abraham Lincoln became president, several southern states seceded. On April 12, 1861, the Civil War began when soldiers fired shots at Fort Sumter, South Carolina. Over the next four years, the North and South battled in a bloody, bitter war. Eventually, the North prevailed and the war ended in April 1865. That same year, Congress passed the Thirteenth Amendment to the U.S. Constitution that formally abolished slavery across the United States. Slaves rejoiced. Their long-awaited freedom was at hand.

After the initial excitement, the reality of freedom became clear. Approximately 4 million slaves were now free people. Most of them, however, were poor and illiterate. Many were also homeless after being thrown off slaveholders' lands. The newly freed slaves had few skills or resources to live independently. To survive, many took jobs that were similar to tasks they performed on antebellum plantations. They became caterers, butchers, barbers, and delivery men. Eventually, black athletes turned to sports as a way to make a living and escape poverty.

America's First National Sport: Horse Racing

In the 1800s quarter-horse racing was popular in the United States. As the interest in horse racing grew, the demand for workers to race, train, and care for horses also grew. Caring for horses was a labor-intensive job that many whites did not want. For years black workers and slaves had tended horses on farms and plantations. Owners realized that slaves who were familiar with horses had the best chance of winning races. Slaves became the leading horse trainers, groomers, and jockeys in antebellum America.

The first Kentucky Derby, in 1875, was won by African American jockey Oliver Lewis.

After the Civil War ended, horse racing exploded in popularity. Towns around the country built racetracks. Newly freed black jockeys and trainers discovered that they could use their horse skills to make a living. While many other blacks had little hope of improving their station in life, horse racing gave jockeys, trainers, and groomers an opportunity to make their lives better.

In 1875 the first Kentucky Derby was held. On race day the *Louisville Courier-Journal* wrote, "Today will be history for Kentucky annals as the first 'Derby Day' of what promises to be a long series of annual festivities, which we confidently expect our grandchildren a hundred years hence to celebrate in glorious centennial rejoicings."[6] That first Kentucky Derby made history for African Americans as well, when black jockey Oliver Lewis rode a horse named Aristides to victory. In fact, fourteen out of fifteen jockeys in the first derby were black. Through the end of the 1800s, black jockeys won the Kentucky Derby twelve more times.

Isaac Murphy

One of the most famous black derby winners was a jockey named Isaac Murphy. Born in 1861, Murphy was the son of free black parents. After his father's death in the Civil War, Murphy and his mother moved to Lexington, Kentucky. Young Murphy often came with his mother to her job at a racing stable. At the stables, a trainer noticed Murphy because of his small size and began training him as a jockey. Five days after the first Kentucky Derby, fourteen-year-old Murphy made his racing debut.

A few months later Murphy won his first race. By the end of 1876, Murphy had won eleven races. In 1877 he won nineteen races and rode in his first Kentucky Derby. A few years later Murphy rode to his first victory in the 1884 Kentucky Derby.

Murphy's exceptional riding talent made him one of the most desirable jockeys in racing. Owners wanted Murphy to ride their horses. In 1890 and 1891 Murphy won the derby again, becoming the first jockey to win the Kentucky Derby three times. In 1884 Murphy also won the American Derby in Chicago, the most prestigious race of the time. He would win this race three more times, in 1885, 1886, and 1888.

Murphy's remarkable success in the Kentucky Derby and other prominent national races led many to call him the greatest black athlete of the nineteenth century. In addition, Murphy rode to victory in a remarkable 44 percent of his races, a feat that is still admired today.

Segregation Lines Harden

While black jockeys were winning races, the black community struggled to survive in the South. After the war, many southern whites returned to their old ways. The slaves might have been free, but whites still treated them as inferior beings. Around 1865 many southern states started passing laws known as Black Codes. These laws limited the freedom of blacks. They restricted where blacks could work and live and even whom they could marry.

The Civil Rights Act of 1866 tried to overrule the Black Codes. Unfortunately, whites controlled the southern police, courts, and legislatures. They intimidated blacks from even trying to assert their legal rights. Too often, if a former slave brought a complaint to the court, the case was simply ignored.

Violence against blacks also increased. White mobs beat blacks and destroyed their property for minor offenses. Kidnappings, murders, and lynching were common. During this time secret organized groups like the Ku Klux Klan formed. They terrorized blacks to keep them from challenging white power.

By the late 1800s conditions for blacks were steadily getting worse. Segregation was on the rise. In 1883 the Supreme Court overturned the Civil Rights Act of 1875 that forbade discrimination in hotels, trains, and other public places. Then in 1896 the Supreme Court ruled in *Plessy v. Ferguson* to uphold "separate but equal" laws. This decision made it acceptable for states to have separate facilities for the two races. As a result, many communities segregated virtually all areas of public life. Blacks and whites had separate schools, restrooms, theaters, and restaurants. Unfortunately, the separate facilities were rarely equal. The areas set aside for blacks were usually inferior to those for whites.

White Jockeys Challenge Traditional Roles

At first, white riders did not challenge black jockeys, because they did not want jobs traditionally held by blacks. However, as Murphy and other black riders made racing more popular, the money in horse racing increased. By the 1880s riding horses became a way for disadvantaged young men of all races to move upward socially and economically.

Jim Crow Laws

After the federal troops left the South in 1877, former slaveholding white southerners returned to power in state and local government. Almost immediately, they passed laws to segregate the races. These laws were called Jim Crow laws, named after a popular nineteenth-century minstrel song that stereotyped blacks. While Jim Crow laws differed in each state, they shared similar characteristics. Jim Crow laws restricted where blacks could live, go to school, and worship. They required blacks to use separate public facilities. The laws also limited which jobs blacks could take. Like the earlier Black Codes, Jim Crow laws tried to block blacks from voting through literacy tests that were difficult or impossible to pass or taxes they could not afford to pay.

Some Jim Crow laws forced blacks to act subservient to whites. Blacks had to tip their hats to whites as they passed on the street. They were expected to step out of the way for whites on the sidewalk. In stores black customers had to wait patiently to be served after whites, if they were served at all. Blacks also had to address whites with respectful titles like "sir" and "ma'am." Whites, on the other hand, called adult blacks "boy" and "girl." Even worse, many whites simply used offensive racial slurs whenever talking to blacks.

As discrimination and segregation increased, bands of white jockeys formed "anti-colored" unions in the 1890s. These groups attempted to force black jockeys off the track. They would gang up on black jockeys during races, ensuring that they did not win. According to a 1900 Chicago newspaper account, "a black boy would be pocketed, thrust back in the race; or his mount would be bumped out of contention; or a white boy would run along-side, slip a foot under a black boy's stirrup and toss him out of the saddle. Again while ostensibly whipping their own horses those white fellows would slash out and cut the nearest Negro rider. They nearly ran the black boys off the tracks."[7]

The Jockey Club

In 1894 white riders established the Jockey Club. The club became the administrative organization for the horse racing industry. One of its new responsibilities was to license jockeys. If a jockey was not licensed, he could not ride in organized horse races. When the club restricted the number of black jockeys it licensed, it effectively reduced their numbers in the sport.

Licensed black jockeys also received fewer invitations to ride horses. Owners feared white jockeys would gang up against a black rider on the track, making sure he did not win a race. Fewer mounts to ride and the roadblocks to obtaining a racing license caused the number of black jockeys in the United States to drop dramatically. While a few black jockeys still managed to have some success in big stakes races, most could no longer make a living in the United States. Instead, black jockeys headed to Europe, where they could still ride and make a living. By the 1930s less than 1 percent of licensed jockeys were black. Even Isaac Murphy was affected by the increasing white presence on the track. He was out of racing entirely by the early 1890s.

Boxing Obstacles

Before the Civil War, boxing was a popular form of entertainment on southern plantations. Slaves and owners watched matches that pitted slave against slave. Often the crowd wagered on the outcome. Talented slaves could win a fortune for white owners who bet on a match and won.

After the war's end, black boxers used their talents to make a living. Still, they struggled against a rule that prevented them from fighting for the heavyweight championship. While white boxers would fight blacks on the way to the crown, once they achieved boxing prominence, they refused to fight matches against black opponents.

Peter Jackson was one of the most famous nineteenth-century black boxers. Born in the West Indies, Jackson began his boxing career in 1882 in Australia. In 1886 he won the Australian heavyweight title by knocking out white boxer Tom Leeds. Following his victory Jackson moved to the United States in 1888. He found that white fighters were reluctant to face him. Instead he fought another black boxer, George Godfrey, and won the world black heavyweight championship.

As the new black heavyweight champion, Jackson found white fighters were more willing to fight him. They hoped that by defeating

Peter Jackson was one of the nineteenth century's best black boxers. He never competed for the heavyweight title because the reigning champion, John L. Sullivan, refused to fight him because of his color.

Tom Molineaux

■

Tom Molineaux was born a slave in Virginia in 1784. Trained by his father, Molineaux fought fellow slaves while plantation owners bet on the matches. After beating a rival plantation's slave, he earned a significant sum for his owner. The owner gave Molineaux his freedom and five hundred dollars.

In 1809 Molineaux left the United States and sailed to England. He worked with trainer Bill Richmond, another freed American slave who had become a prizefighter in England. His impressive bare-knuckle boxing performances led to a title match against British heavyweight champion Tom Cribb.

In December 1810 Molineaux faced Cribb. Most people expected Cribb to win easily. However, Molineaux proved to be a smart and powerful boxer. The fight lasted thirty-nine rounds, with Cribb being declared the winner. Although he lost, Molineaux astonished and impressed fans with his powerful hitting, strength, and skill. In 1811 Molineaux and Cribb fought for a second time. This time Cribb retained his title with an eleventh-round knockout.

After the Cribb fights, Molineaux became a celebrity in England. He fought other bouts and exhibitions. In 1814 he defeated boxer William Fuller in two rounds, which lasted over an hour. Molineaux died in 1818.

This nineteenth-century illustration depicts the boxing match between Tom Molineaux (third from right) and Tom Cribb.

Jackson, they could set up their own title fights for the world heavyweight championship. For his part Jackson hoped that if he defeated respected white fighters, he might also have a chance to fight for the world heavyweight championship.

In 1890 John L. Sullivan was the world heavyweight champion. Although several athletic clubs made lucrative offers to host a fight between Sullivan and Jackson, Sullivan refused to fight Jackson because of his color. For years Jackson unsuccessfully tried to set up a title fight. He retired in 1892 and attempted a brief comeback in 1898. Jackson died in 1901 from tuberculosis. He never had the chance to prove in the ring that he was the world's best.

Major Taylor: The "Colored Cyclone"

Although Jackson was denied the opportunity to fight for boxing's ultimate prize, other nineteenth-century black athletes were able to reach the heights of their respective sports. A young black man named Marshall "Major" Taylor overcame prejudice and discrimination to become the premier bicycle rider of the day.

In the late 1800s the cycling craze spread across America. By 1890 there were more than one hundred thousand cyclists in the United States. Nearly every town had cycling clubs for whites, blacks, women, and children. Soon bicycling became an organized sport. Velodromes, or bike racing arenas, were constructed across the United States. Fans came to watch cyclists race around the tracks at top speed.

Born in rural Indiana, Major Taylor received his first bicycle from a wealthy white family that employed his father as a coachman. In 1892 a local bike shop in Indianapolis, Indiana, hired him to perform cycling stunts outside the shop. He earned the nickname "Major" because he wore a soldier's uniform as a costume during the performances. Taylor worked in bicycle shops and was guided by Birdie Munger, a former cycling star. Under Munger's tutoring, Taylor was introduced to professional cycling. He won his first race in 1892 at age thirteen.

In 1894 the League of American Wheelmen, bicycling's governing body, banned blacks from amateur racing. Yet Taylor proved his talent competing in races against other black cyclists to become the black cycling champion.

When Munger moved to Worcester, Massachusetts, in 1895 to open a bicycle factory, Taylor moved with him. He found Worcester a more accepting place to train. "I was in Worcester only a very short time before I realized that there was no such race prejudice existing among the bicycle riders there as I had experienced in Indianapolis,"[8] Taylor wrote in his autobiography, *The Fastest Bicycle Rider in the World.*

By 1896 Taylor broke two world track records for paced and unpaced mile rides on an Indianapolis track. In retaliation for his success, whites banned him from Indianapolis's Capital City track. Yet Taylor's sprinting speed proved he was ready to ride in professional races. A New York racing board that opposed the color ban agreed to register him as a pro.

Taylor's feats soon became legendary. From 1898 to 1904 he was the fastest bicycle rider in the world. By 1898 he held seven world records in his specialty—sprint races. In 1899 Taylor won the world 1-mile (1.6km) championship in Montreal, Canada. The following year Taylor completed the national championship series and was crowned the American sprint champion.

Despite his success Taylor faced many challenges because of his color. In 1897 many southern race promoters would not allow him to enter their races. When he was allowed to race, people along the route tried to sabotage him. Some shoved sticks in his wheels as he rode past. In addition, white riders often abused and threatened him. In one race a competitor pulled Taylor from his bike and choked him until he was unconscious. In Atlanta he was warned to leave town within forty-eight hours. In some cities, such as St. Louis, Missouri, and San Francisco, California, hotel managers refused him lodging.

In 1901 Taylor signed with the European bike tour and beat every European champion. From 1902 to 1904 Taylor competed in races in Europe, Australia, New Zealand, and the United States. He became known as the fastest bicyclist in the world. When Taylor retired in 1910 at age thirty-two, he had won hundreds of races and was an international star.

Moses Fleetwood Walker

In 1869 the first professional baseball team formed, and in 1871 the first professional league formed. Between the end of the Civil

Major Taylor held seven world records in bicycling, but in 1894 blacks were banned from amateur competition in the United States. Taylor was forced to spend most of his career racing in Europe.

War and 1890, a number of black athletes played on white, minor league teams. While many only played for a brief time because of local prejudice and unofficial color bans, a few black athletes had successful careers in professional baseball.

Moses Fleetwood Walker became the first black athlete to play in Major League Baseball. In 1883 Walker signed as a catcher with the minor league Toledo Blue Stockings of the Northwestern League. A year later the Toledo, Ohio, team joined the American Association, which was considered a major league at the time. Walker played forty-two games for Toledo in 1884 at which time he was joined by his brother Weldy Walker, who would play just six games for the short-handed team. Yet even on his own

In 1881 Moses Walker, labeled number six, and his brother Weldy, number ten, pose with the first varsity baseball team at Oberlin College. Three years later the brothers would become the first blacks to play Major League Baseball.

John Shippen Jr.

John Shippen Jr. is known as the first African American professional golfer. He played in the U.S. Open championship five times but was denied participation in many other tournaments because of his race.

Long before African American golfing great Tiger Woods made headlines, John Shippen Jr. became the first African American professional golfer. In 1896 Shippen entered the U.S. Golf Association's U.S. Open tournament at the new Shinnecock Hills Golf Club. When white golfers discovered that Shippen was scheduled to play, they threatened to boycott the tournament. Theodore Havemeyer, the U.S. Golf Association president, supported Shippen's right to play. He announced that the Open would take place even if Shippen and Oscar Bunn, a Native American golfer, were the only two playing.

As a result, Shippen and Bunn became the first American-born golfers to play in the Open. In that event, Shippen tied for fifth place. Over the rest of his career, he golfed in four more U.S. Open tournaments. He was frequently denied the opportunity to play in other tournaments because of his race. Still, Shippen remained committed to golf and became a golf professional at several clubs over his career.

team, Moses Walker encountered discrimination. Toledo team-mate and pitcher Tony Mullane refused to take signals from him. "[Moses] Walker was the best catcher I ever worked with . . . but whenever I had to pitch to him I used to pitch anything I wanted without looking at his signals," said Mullane. "He caught me and caught anything I pitched without knowing what was coming."[9] Moses Walker did not last long in the majors. In July 1884 he broke a rib during a game and was released by Toledo. He spent the next five years playing for other teams and leagues.

Despite his efforts, Moses Walker was never able to get back into the major leagues. In the 1880s baseball salaries had begun to rise. Roster spots were extremely competitive. Baseball executives realized that if black players were allowed to compete, they would take jobs away from white players. In 1887 owners in the International League, the most prestigious minor league circuit, voted not to hand out future contracts to black players. Later the International League agreed to limit black players to one per team. By 1889, Walker's last season in baseball, he was the last black player in the International League.

When the 1890 season began, there were no black players in the International League. For a few short years, black baseball players could still find work in less-prestigious leagues, but soon no team in white organized baseball would accept black players. By 1900 the Major League Baseball color line was firmly drawn. It would not be broken for almost half a century. In the meantime African American athletes would have to find new places to compete.

Chapter Two

Playing in Separate Leagues

In 1895 Booker T. Washington stood at the Cotton States and International Exposition in Atlanta, Georgia, and delivered his famous "Atlanta Compromise" speech. A prominent spokesperson for the black community, Washington said, "In all things that are purely social we can be as separate as the fingers, yet one as the hand in all things essential to mutual progress."[10] By 1900 most of America was as divided as Washington described. Racial segregation was an accepted practice. Blacks and whites had separate schools, restrooms, theaters, and restaurants. Unfortunately, the separate facilities were rarely equal. The areas set aside for blacks were usually inferior to those for whites.

In this environment many sporting leagues closed their doors to black athletes. No matter how talented they were, black athletes were not allowed to compete with whites. Forced out of white leagues, African American athletes established separate sporting leagues and teams. These leagues became a home for players excluded from white sports.

Baseball's Negro Leagues

One of the most famous African American leagues in the early twentieth century was baseball's Negro leagues. As black baseball

CUBAN GIANTS 3 – WORCESTER 2 – JULY 22 – 16

The first black professional baseball team, the Cuban Giants, plays a local Worcester, Massachusetts, team in 1916. The Giants traveled the country, taking on any local teams that would play them.

players were forced out of white teams, groups of players formed their own teams.

The first black professional team was the Cuban Giants, organized in 1885. Other teams soon followed. From early spring to late fall, these teams traveled around the country, challenging local teams in small towns and rural areas. They played black or white teams, on sandlots or in major league stadiums. "We played baseball every day," said Arthur W. Hardy, a pitcher on the Topeka, Kansas, Giants from 1906 to 1912. "We started in Topeka and we played up through Kansas, Iowa, and into Illinois and Chicago. And then we played back in those little country towns."[11] By the end of the nineteenth century, all-black baseball teams were commonplace.

Between 1900 and 1920, many famous black baseball teams were formed. These included the Chicago American Giants, the New York Lincoln Giants, and the Homestead Grays. Rivalries between the teams were intense. Because independent teams had no league or tournament to crown a champion, any team could claim to hold the title of world champion of the black teams. If they did so, they were usually challenged by another team to play for the championship. While some teams were successful, such as the Kansas City Monarchs or the Chicago American Giants, others like the Cleveland Hornets lasted only a season or two.

Rube Foster Organizes the Negro National League

By the end of World War I, black baseball was a popular entertainment attraction for urban black populations across the country. In 1920 Andrew "Rube" Foster, the manager of the Chicago American Giants, proposed a national association for the Negro baseball clubs. Foster was tired of teams stealing each other's

Andrew "Rube" Foster organized the first black baseball league, the Negro National League. He was voted into the Baseball Hall of Fame in 1981.

players. "If you have taken your club east, (and) win many games, the owners try to take the men away from you, bring dissatisfaction between you and your men; so much so you avoid going there,"[12] he wrote in the *Chicago Defender*, a popular black newspaper.

In Kansas City, Missouri, Foster and the owners of the top midwestern black teams met and formed the Negro National League. The league initially had eight teams. On May 2, 1920, the Indianapolis ABCs defeated the Chicago Giants in the Negro National League's first game. Soon rival leagues formed in the East and the South. Led by Foster, the Negro National League continued for most of the 1920s. It fell victim to the Great Depression, the grave economic decline that hit the United States in 1929, and dissolved after the 1931 season.

A Second Negro National League

In 1931 Pittsburgh tavern owner Gus Greenlee organized the Pittsburgh Crawfords. Although he did not have a baseball background, Greenlee had a stacked wallet to pay a lineup of great players, including Satchel Paige, Josh Gibson, Oscar Charleston, Judy Johnson, Cool Papa Bell, Ted Page, Leroy Matlock, and Jimmie Crutchfield. After Foster's Negro National League folded, Greenlee organized a second Negro National League in 1933. Greenlee's league soon became the driving force behind black baseball through 1949. Two other leagues, the Negro Southern League and the Negro American League, also formed and became Negro National League rivals.

Despite the economic downturn of the Great Depression, the three major Negro leagues prospered. Unlike earlier Negro leagues, the second Negro National League stood on solid financial ground. Through the 1930s and early 1940s, most clubs at least broke even. During World War II Negro league baseball grew to be a $2 million per year business. Together, the Negro leagues became one of the largest and most successful black-owned organizations in the United States.

Josh Gibson: The "Black Babe Ruth"

The Negro leagues were home to many legendary baseball players. One of the greatest was Josh Gibson, a right-handed slugger nicknamed the "black Babe Ruth." In the batter's box, Gibson excited crowds. Every time he stepped to the plate, fans expected

Paul Robeson

■

Attending Rutgers University in 1915 on a full academic scholarship, Paul Robeson excelled in sports. He earned fifteen varsity letters in football, baseball, basketball, and track and field. In football he was named a first-team All-American twice. As the school's first African American football player, he endured discrimination. His locker was segregated from the rest of the team's. When the team traveled, Robeson stayed in black-only hotel rooms. During his freshman year Robeson was banned from the annual football banquet.

Sometimes Robeson also faced physical injury. In one scrimmage teammates hit Robeson so hard that he left with two broken ribs, a dislocated shoulder, and a broken nose. Another time, a player stepped on his hand with such force that his cleats ripped off Robeson's fingernails.

Despite the treatment, Robeson became a spectacular player. After college he played professional football for a few years and used his salary to pay for law school. Eventually, Robeson quit football to become a lawyer. After a few years he discovered that the arts provided the best opportunity to express himself. Always outspoken against racial injustice, he left law to promote African and African American history and culture in theater and music. Famous around the world, Robeson became an acclaimed actor and singer.

his swing to crack a home run ball, each farther than the last. "It was just a treat to watch him hit the ball. There was no effort at all,"[13] said Judy Johnson, one of Gibson's first managers.

Born in 1911, Gibson started playing ball as a teenager for a semipro team. When he was eighteen, Gibson attended a Negro league game between the Homestead Grays and Kansas City Monarchs. When Homestead's catcher injured his hand, the manager, who had heard of Gibson's reputation, went looking in the stands for Gibson. "I asked him if he wanted to catch and he said 'yes, sir,' so we had to hold up the game while he went and put on Buck Ewing's uniform," Johnson said. "We signed him the next day."[14]

Gibson quickly became a Negro league star. Over his seventeen-year career, he was credited with hitting almost eight hundred home runs. He won nine home run titles and four batting crowns while playing for the Pittsburgh Crawfords and Homestead Grays. It is also reported that in the late 1930s, Gibson's batting average rose above .400.

Gibson's home runs were known for being spectacularly deep. He often sent balls flying more than 500 feet (152m). One homer was reportedly measured at 575 feet (175m). Some reports say that Gibson hit a fair ball out of New York's Yankee Stadium, the only hitter ever to do so.

It was reported that two major league teams, the Washington Senators and Pittsburgh Pirates, considered giving Gibson a try-out in the late 1930s. Despite the rumors, the tryout never occurred. Instead, Gibson played his entire career in the Negro leagues. He died at the age of thirty-five, in 1947, three months before Jackie Robinson made his debut with the Brooklyn Dodgers. Years after his death baseball recognized Gibson's great career. In 1972 he became the second African American player inducted into the National Baseball Hall of Fame.

Leroy "Satchel" Paige

Pitcher Leroy "Satchel" Paige dominated Negro league baseball from the late 1930s through the mid-1940s. His pitching was legendary, and his showboating entertained legions of fans. Hall of Famer Joe DiMaggio said that Satchel Paige was the best and fastest pitcher he ever faced. Over a five-decade career, Paige recorded feats such as sixty-four consecutive scoreless innings and a twenty-one-game winning streak. He threw more pitches, usually strikes, for more seasons than any pitcher past or present.

Nicknamed "Satchel" after working as a baggage carrier, Paige joined the Negro Southern League in 1926. Soon everyone was talking about the tall, lanky pitcher. "With the Birmingham [Alabama] ball club, the only big thing we had was Satchel," said teammate Jimmie Crutchfield. "Everybody in the South knew about Satchel Paige, even then. We'd have 8,000 people out— sometimes more—when he was pitching, which was something in Birmingham."[15]

Pitching for the Pittsburgh Crawfords off and on from 1932 to 1937, Paige recorded impressive records of 23–7 in 1932 and 31–4 in 1933. He was also reported to have pitched twenty-one straight wins and sixty-four consecutive scoreless innings. During the off season, Paige played in Mexico, South America, or the Caribbean. He also traveled around the country in exhibition games against the white major leaguers.

Paige's most famous pitch was the hesitation pitch. When throwing it, Paige deliberately paused when his left foot hit the ground. Over six exhibition games in 1934 to 1935, Paige beat baseball's best white pitcher of the time, Dizzy Dean, 4–2. "My fastball looks like a change of pace alongside that pistol bullet old Satch shoots up to the plate," Dean said. "If Satch and I were pitching on the same team, we'd clinch the pennant by the fourth of July and go fishing until World Series time."[16] As a Negro league star, Paige made as much as forty thousand dollars per year, more than any other African American player at the time.

In 1947 a young player named Jackie Robinson broke the color line in Major League Baseball, which had been firmly drawn in

Josh Gibson, right, hit almost eight-hundred home runs in his career. Satchel Paige, left, over a five-decade career, threw more pitches for more seasons than any pitcher in history. Both are in the Baseball Hall of Fame.

James "Cool Papa" Bell

For more than twenty years, James "Cool Papa" Bell was known as the fastest man in baseball. A speedster on the bases, Bell reportedly circled the diamond in twelve seconds. His speed made him a threat anytime he set foot on the diamond. An amazing base stealer, he once stole two bases in a single pitch. He was also said to have been so fast that he once scored from first base after the hitter laid down an infield bunt. According to teammate Satchel Paige, if colleges had known about Cool Papa Bell, Olympic runner Jesse Owens would have looked like he was walking!

Bell started his career as an outfielder and pitcher for the St. Louis Stars in 1922. After ten years he joined the great Pittsburgh Crawfords, joining four future Hall of Famers. In a career that spanned more than twenty years, Bell played for three of the greatest teams in the Negro leagues: the Pittsburgh Crawfords, Homestead Grays, and St. Louis Stars, winning several championships. When baseball integrated in the late 1940s, however, it was too late for Bell. His legs were gone. In 1974 Bell was inducted into the National Baseball Hall of Fame.

Cool Papa Bell, second from left in the back row, poses with the 1943 Homestead Grays. His career spanned twenty years, and in 1974 he was elected to baseball's Hall of Fame.

1900. Paige was also given a chance in the big leagues when the Cleveland Indians needed a pitcher for the 1948 pennant race. At age forty-two, he became the first African American pitcher in Major League Baseball and helped his team win the pennant. After pitching with the Indians for two seasons, Paige played for St. Louis and Kansas City. Over his major league career, he posted a 28–31 record with a 3.29 earned run average.

Paige's longevity was astounding. In 1965 a fifty-nine-year-old Paige threw three scoreless innings for Kansas City. When asked about his age, Paige became famous for saying, "Age is a question of mind over matter. If you don't mind, it doesn't matter."[17] Finally, in 1971, the ageless Satchel Paige was given a place in history as the first Negro league star elected to Major League Baseball's Hall of Fame.

On the Court: New York Renaissance

While black baseball players entertained crowds in the Negro leagues, one of basketball's first true dynasties formed in 1922. The all-black New York Renaissance (nicknamed the Rens) played teams across the country, winning more than two thousand games during their twenty-five years in existence. Because professional basketball leagues would not accept a black team, the Rens barnstormed across the country, showcasing their skills and fancy passes. The Rens played all types of teams, from semi-pro squads to black college and other professional teams. They handily defeated many opponents. During one stretch in 1932–1933, the Rens won an amazing eighty-eight straight games. "To this day, I have never seen a team play better team basketball," said Hall of Fame coach John Wooden, who played against the Rens when he was a member of the barnstorming Indianapolis Kautskys during the 1930s. "They had great athletes, but they weren't as impressive as their team play. The way they handled and passed the ball was just amazing to me then, and I believe it would be today."[18]

One of the Rens' most famous opponents was another New York team and the premier team of the era, the Original Celtics. Games between the Rens and Celtics were popular. Some were attended by as many as fifteen thousand fans. While the Celtics were the benchmark team of the 1920s, the Rens quickly joined them in the 1930s. In the early 1930s the Rens beat the Original Celtics for the world basketball championship. Some of the Rens players credited their competition with the Celtics for helping them become a better team. "The Rens learned a lot from the Celtics," said John Isaacs, a Rens player from 1936 to 1941. "They played with their heads. And when we played other teams, we instituted a lot of their stuff—playing smart basketball, setting each other up. . . . They were good teachers and, after a while, the student started taking it to the teacher."[19]

Despite the Rens' success on the court, the professional basketball leagues refused again, in 1946, to admit the Rens. Eventually, in 1949, the Rens disbanded. "I was raised hearing that the Celtics were the greatest team of all time," said Richard Lapchick, son of Celtics center Joe Lapchick. "My dad's friends would say that and all our neighbors would say that. But he would correct them and say, 'The Rens were every bit as good as we were in the beginning and were better than us in the end.'"[20]

Jack Johnson

Although most black athletes played in separate leagues during the early 1900s, some successfully participated in predominantly white sports. Born in 1878 in Texas, Jack Johnson began boxing as a teenager. At the time, black boxers could compete for some titles, but not for the world heavyweight championship.

For fourteen years Johnson boxed and built his reputation and wealth by winning matches against black and white fighters. Looking to fight the best in the world, Jack Johnson repeatedly challenged James J. Jeffries, the heavyweight champion, to a match. However, Jeffries refused to box Johnson. Instead, he retired undefeated.

In 1908 Johnson's chance at the title came when the new heavyweight champion, Tommy Burns, agreed to fight him. At a match in Australia, Johnson beat the white Burns to become the first African American heavyweight champion of the world. According to Johnson biographer Randy Roberts, whites found Johnson's win hard to take. "The press reacted [to Johnson's victory] as if Armageddon [the end of the world] was here. That this may be the moment when it all starts to fall apart for white society,"[21] Roberts said.

During the "Battle of the Century" on July 4, 1920, in Reno, Nevada, African American Jack Johnson knocked out James Jeffries, who was white, in the fifteenth round. Race riots erupted across the country.

Out of the boxing ring, Johnson's public image upset many whites. He wore fancy clothes, drove flashy cars, and openly dated and married white women. Angry whites accused the black man of acting above his station. "Johnson ruptured role after role set aside for Negroes in American society,"[22] said historian Lawrence Levine.

Some refused to acknowledge Johnson as the world heavyweight champion. They unsuccessfully tried to match him against white boxers, called "great white hopes," to take back the title. Finally, boxing promoters convinced former champion James J. Jeffries to come out of retirement to fight Johnson. Promoted as the "Battle of the Century," the fight took place on July 4, 1910, in Reno, Nevada. After Johnson downed Jeffries in the fifteenth round, deadly race riots erupted across the country. To prevent more violence, Congress passed an act that banned the interstate transport of fight films. They feared that films of Johnson beating white boxers would cause more violence.

In 1913 Johnson fled the United States after being convicted of transporting a white woman across state lines for immoral purposes. The trial was considered by many to be questionable. He spent several years in Europe. In 1915 he lost his title to boxer Jess Willard in Cuba. Rumors flew that Johnson threw the fight in an attempt to placate authorities and return to the United States. In 1920 he finally returned to the United States and spent eight months in federal prison. After his release, he boxed a few more matches but retired in 1928. Johnson died in a car crash in 1946.

While Johnson may have been one of the best fighters to step into the ring, he may be remembered more for his flamboyant style and controversial actions. "Johnson in many ways is an embodiment of the African-American struggle to be truly free in this country —economically, socially and politically," says filmmaker Ken Burns, who chronicled Johnson's story in the 2005 film *Unforgivable Blackness: The Rise and Fall of Jack Johnson*. "He absolutely refused to play by the rules set by the white establishment, or even those of the black community. In that sense, he fought for freedom not just as a black man, but as an individual."[23] Despite his athletic success, Johnson was never embraced by white Americans. Twenty years later, another boxer named Joe Louis would win the hearts of Americans, black and white.

Joe Louis: The "Brown Bomber"

Born Joseph Louis Barrow in 1914, Louis started boxing at the request of a schoolmate. After winning fifty out of fifty-four amateur bouts, Louis turned pro in 1934. As a professional he won his first twenty-seven fights, twenty-three of them by knockout. His undefeated streak ended in 1936 when German boxer Max Schmeling beat him.

After his first professional loss, Louis returned to training with one mission—to defeat Schmeling. In the meantime Louis knocked out James Braddock in 1937 and claimed the world heavyweight championship. Louis's powerful performances in the boxing ring made him a hero to the black community. "Every Negro boy old enough to walk wanted to be the next Brown Bomber,"[24] said Malcolm X, then the leader of the militant Black Muslims, an African American religious movement.

The following year, in a rematch against Schmeling, Louis cemented his status as a hero. At the time Adolf Hitler and the National Socialist, or Nazi, Party in Germany were rising to power. For Americans Schmeling was a Nazi figurehead, representing Hitler and the Nazi movement. Louis, on the other hand, represented the United States and democracy. Before the bout, Louis was invited to the White House, where President Franklin Roosevelt told him that the United States needed muscles like his to beat Germany.

At New York's Yankee Stadium, Louis knocked Schmeling to the mat three times in front of a crowd of seventy thousand. Within two minutes, the "Brown Bomber" had knocked out his rival, winning the match. In the process, Louis became a hero that Americans could celebrate. "What my father did was enable white America to think of him as an American, not as a black," said his son, Joe Louis Jr. "By winning, he became white America's first black hero."[25]

Unlike Johnson, Louis carefully cultivated his image outside the ring. "Don't be another Jack Johnson," black fans urged him. Louis's managers made a list of rules to shape his image. The rules included never being photographed with a white woman, never gloating in victory over a white boxer, and never showing emotion in public.

Louis also won over Americans with his patriotism during wartime. When the United States entered World War II, Louis

Joe Louis pummels Max Schmeling to the canvas during their second fight in 1938. Louis was the first black athlete considered a hero by many white Americans, and his triumphs were celebrated by whites and blacks alike.

enlisted in the army. He fought exhibition matches to raise money and boost troop morale. He also donated some of his winnings to military relief funds. "Joe Louis set a stunning example through his acts of patriotism, and even the South responded appreciatively,"[26] said historian Jeffrey Sammons.

Louis held the world heavyweight title for twelve years, the longest that any boxer has ever held the title. He won twenty-four bouts during that time. In 1949 Louis retired undefeated. Upon his death in 1981, Louis was buried in Arlington National Cemetery at the request of President Ronald Reagan, an honor predominantly reserved for former U.S. military members.

Jesse Owens and the 1936 Olympics

In the 1930s black Americans were treated as second-class citizens. Yet when facing Nazi Germany, Americans put aside their differences to unify behind national pride. In 1936 a young black track star named Jesse Owens electrified the country with his record-setting four-gold-medal performance at the Olympic Games. The young black man became America's greatest national track hero.

Born the son of an Alabama cotton picker, James Cleveland Owens quickly became a high school track star. Although he set records for the broad jump and 100-yard dash, he was not offered a college scholarship. Nevertheless, Owens enrolled at Ohio State University. His fleet-footed performances earned him national recognition. As a sophomore, he obliterated the best college athletes at the 1935 Big Ten track-and-field championships. In a single meet, Owen bested three world records and tied a fourth.

While Owens was smashing track records, Nazism was growing in Germany. The world was on the verge of World War II. The 1936 Olympics were scheduled to be held in Berlin, Germany. German leader Hitler believed the Olympics would be a world stage for his athletes to demonstrate their superiority. To his dismay, Owens, an African American descended from slaves, ran and jumped for four gold medals in the 100- and 200-meter dashes, the long jump, and the 4x100-relay team. He became the first American track-and-field athlete to win four gold medals in a single Olympic Games. His performances thrilled the world and unified Americans.

Jesse Owens won four gold medals in the 1936 Olympic Games in Berlin, Germany.

After the Games, Owens returned home to a New York ticker tape parade. Despite his spectacular performances, however, Owens encountered discrimination in his own country. For a reception being held in his honor at New York's Waldorf-Astoria Hotel, Owens was asked to ride the freight elevator. The irony did not go unnoticed by Owens. "When I came back to my native country, after all the stories about Hitler, I couldn't ride in the front of the bus," Owens said. "I had to go to the back door. I couldn't live where I wanted. I wasn't invited to shake hands with Hitler, but I wasn't invited to the White House to shake hands with the President, either."[27]

Unlike today's Olympic stars, Owens did not make money from endorsements after the Games either. Instead, he worked a variety of jobs, including running races against horses and dogs. "People said it was degrading for an Olympic champion to run

Tuskegee Women's Track and Field

In 1929 one of the first competitive women's track teams began at the all-black Tuskegee Institute (known today as Tuskegee University). The school immediately added women's events to its Tuskegee Relays, the first major track meet sponsored by a black college. The team became the premier women's track team in the 1930s and 1940s and won eleven Amateur Athletic Union outdoor championships between 1937 and 1948. Tuskegee star Alice Coachman became the first black woman to take home Olympic gold, winning the high jump in the 1948 Olympics.

against a horse, but what was I supposed to do?" Owens said. "I had four gold medals, but you can't eat four gold medals."[28]

Owens used his fame to travel as an inspirational speaker, addressing youth groups, professional organizations, sports banquets, and many other groups and events. He also devoted much of his time to working with underprivileged youth, becoming a board member and director of the Chicago Boys Club.

In February 1979 President Jimmy Carter presented Owens with the Living Legend Award. "A young man who possibly didn't even realize the superb nature of his own capabilities went to the Olympics and performed in a way that I don't believe has ever been equaled since . . . and since this superb achievement, he has continued in his own dedicated but modest way to inspire others to reach for greatness,"[29] Carter said about Owens.

As World War II ended, calls for social justice resonated throughout the country. African Americans had proved themselves on the battlefield and in and on ball fields, basketball courts, boxing rings, and tracks across the country. It was time for the color barrier in sports to come crashing down.

Chapter Three

Breaking the Color Line

On December 7, 1941, Japanese planes bombed the U.S. Naval Base at Pearl Harbor in Hawaii. With this, the United States entered World War II with a flurry of patriotism. Yet the black community was keenly aware of the country's hypocrisy. The United States fought for democracy in Europe but still allowed Jim Crow laws and discrimination at home. Led by the black press, African Americans protested discrimination in society like no other time in history.

Wendell Smith's Mighty Pen

The *Pittsburgh Courier* was one of the most prominent black newspapers in the 1940s. The paper was well known for its top-notch sports coverage. Sportswriter Wendell Smith was one of the *Courier*'s most influential journalists in the 1930s and 1940s. He used his pen to gain support for Jackie Robinson to become the first black player in Major League Baseball in 1947.

As a teenager Smith experienced the effects of segregated baseball. After Smith pitched a shutout, a game in which the other team does not score a run, a baseball scout passed him over and signed the opposing team's pitcher, who was white. The scout told Smith that he wished he could sign him, but

In February 1948, upon Wendell Smith's recommendation, Brooklyn Dodgers vice president Branch Rickey, at right, signed Jackie Robinson, at left, to a Major League contract. Robinson's signing began the desegregation of Major League Baseball.

could not because of his color. "That's when I decided that if I ever got into a position to do anything, I'd dedicate my life to getting Negro players into the big leagues,"[30] Smith later said.

At the *Courier*, Smith launched a campaign to end segregation in organized baseball. In his columns he protested baseball's segregation. He interviewed eight managers and forty players in the National League about integration. From these interviews Smith wrote a series of articles in 1939 titled "What Big Leaguers Think of Negro Baseball Players." In the interviews only the manager of the New York Giants said that blacks should be banned from organized baseball. The other managers and players said that they would use and play with black players if league officials allowed it.

By the end of the 1930s, the attitudes of some whites had changed toward black Americans. A groundswell of protest in the white community rose over baseball's color line. The *Courier* reported on the increasing criticism from white Americans against baseball's discrimination. World War II gave the paper and Smith even more opportunity to protest the exclusion of black athletes from baseball. As Smith said, "Big league baseball is perpetuating the very things thousands of Americans are overseas fighting to end, namely, racial discrimination and segregation."[31]

Recognizing Smith's efforts to integrate baseball, the president of the Pittsburgh Pirates, William E. Benswanger, reportedly asked Smith in 1942 to recommend a few black players for a tryout with the Pirates. Smith selected four players, including Josh Gibson. Benswanger, however, never followed through with the tryout.

Undeterred, Smith doubled his efforts to break baseball's color line. In the newspaper he blasted Clark Griffith, owner of the Washington Senators, for his opposition to black players. Smith also organized a meeting between the commissioner of organized baseball, Judge Kenesaw Mountain Landis, and the Black Newspaper Publishers Association in December 1943. At the meeting, representatives of the black press argued their case for including black players in the major leagues.

Decline of the Negro Leagues

The signing of Jackie Robinson to the major leagues was a key moment in baseball history. It also signaled the end of baseball's Negro leagues. The best African American baseball players began being recruited for major league teams, and the attention of the African American community followed them. Fans watched the play of Robinson and other African American players and increasingly ignored the Negro league teams, leading to its demise.

In addition, with all the best players moving to major league teams, the talent in the Negro leagues was also shrinking. Young stars such as Willie Mays and Hank Aaron left to play in the majors. A few Negro league teams tried to integrate and add white players to their rosters. Two teams, the Indianapolis Clowns and the Kansas City Monarchs, even added a few female players to attract fans. Despite their efforts, the Negro leagues could no longer earn the money that they had before baseball's integration. In the early 1960s the legendary era came to an end when the last Negro leagues closed.

Nearly a year and a half later, Branch Rickey, a vice president with the Brooklyn Dodgers, decided that he would secretly scout for black players. In April 1945 he asked Smith if he knew of any black players capable of playing in the majors. Smith responded, "If you aren't serious about this, Mr. Rickey, I'd rather not waste our time discussing it, but if you are serious, I do know of a player who could make it. His name is Jackie Robinson."[32] To which Rickey replied, "Jackie Robinson, you say. It seems to me I've heard of that fellow somewhere."[33] The conversation convinced Smith that unlike many white owners before him, Rickey was serious about giving black players an honest tryout. Smith wrote in his column, "It appears to me that Branch Rickey, one of the wisest and shrewdest men in baseball, looms as a valuable friend, both for organized Negro baseball and the cause of the Negro player in the majors."[34]

Jackie Robinson Shatters Baseball's Color Line

In an interview years later, Smith admitted that he did not think that Robinson was the best black ballplayer. Instead, Smith believed Robinson was the right man to join the white major leagues. In college Robinson had played on an integrated team. He excelled at several sports and was one of the greatest all-around athletes at the University of California–Los Angeles (UCLA). "He was the best player at that time for this situation,"[35] explained Smith.

Born in 1919, Jack Roosevelt Robinson grew up in a working-class neighborhood in Pasadena, California. Even as a child he was a fierce competitor, wanting to win whether he played marbles or basketball. At UCLA Robinson became the first athlete to letter in four sports—football, basketball, baseball, and track. He also earned a reputation as a fighter and would reportedly brawl with any white man who insulted him. After college Robinson served in the army during World War II, then joined the Negro league in 1945 as a shortstop for the Kansas City Monarchs.

As Robinson settled into his first season with the Monarchs, Rickey was sending out his scouts, looking for players for his club. Reports came back on several black players, but the name most often mentioned was Robinson's. He, however, was unaware that the eyes of major league scouts watched him.

The glowing reports convinced Rickey that Robinson was his man. Yet he knew that the first black man to cross baseball's color line would have to endure criticism and abuse from fans, competitors, and teammates. He wanted to be sure that Robinson could stand up to the abuse. In August 1945 Rickey met with Robinson in his Brooklyn offices. Robinson thought that he was going to be offered a spot with other black players on Rickey's Negro league team the Brown Dodgers. Instead, Rickey told Robinson that he wanted him to play for the Brooklyn organization. During the interview Rickey described all the insults and abuse Robinson would face. When Robinson asked if Rickey wanted him to fight back, Rickey replied, "I want a ballplayer with guts enough not to fight back. You've got to do this job with base hits and stolen bases and fielding ground balls, Jackie. Nothing else."[36] At the end of the meeting, the two agreed that Robinson would play for the minor league Montreal Royals, the Dodgers' top farm team or training team, in 1946.

Robinson Debuts

Professional baseball's color line cracked on April 18, 1946, when Robinson debuted as the second baseman for the Royals. That season he batted a minor league–leading .349, stole forty bases, and led his team to the Little World Series championship. The following year, on April 15, 1947, Robinson was called up to his first Major League game for the Brooklyn Dodgers.

At first, reaction to Robinson was mixed. Some whites and almost all blacks applauded his joining the team. However, many whites, including many Major League Baseball players, did not think Robinson should play in the majors. Some of his own teammates protested having a black man on the team. Opposing pitchers sometimes threw at his head, while catchers spit on his shoes. One opposing player spiked Robinson with his cleats, opening a large gash in his leg. People in the crowd yelled insults. Robinson and his family even received hate letters and death threats. Bill Nack of *Sports Illustrated* wrote that "Robinson was the target of racial epithets and flying cleats, of hate letters and death threats, of pitchers throwing at his head and legs, and catchers spitting on his shoes."[37]

Yet even as some people harassed Robinson, others supported him. In one memorable moment, as fans harassed Robinson, teammate Pee Wee Reese walked over to Robinson and put his arm around him. When some of Robinson's teammates threatened to sit out rather than play with him, Dodgers manager Leo Durocher told them that he would trade them before he traded Robinson. Other men, including league president Ford Frick, baseball commissioner Happy Chandler, and Jewish baseball star Hank Greenberg, also defended Robinson's right to play in the major leagues.

Through it all, Robinson handled the pressure of being baseball's trailblazer with dignity. He put aside the prejudice and proved how talented he was. In his first year in the majors, Robinson hit twelve home runs, led the National League in stolen bases, and won Rookie of the Year. His play also helped the Dodgers win the National League pennant. During 1949 Robinson hit an impressive .342 batting average, led the league in stolen bases again, and earned the National League's Most Valuable Player Award.

When Branch Rickey (left) signed Jackie Robinson (right), he told him that he needed a ballplayer with the strength not to fight back. Robinson agreed and although he endured years of racial taunts, his actions changed the course of Major League Baseball.

In this memorable photo Dodgers captain Pee Wee Reese holds hands with Jackie Robinson after his home run, as a show of support for Robinson in front of the Dodgers crowd.

Over the next decade with the Dodgers, Robinson helped his team win the National League pennant several times. He was a solid hitter, outstanding base stealer, and a great defensive player. In 1955 Robinson and the Dodgers won baseball's top prize, the World Series.

Eventually, Robinson began to speak out about the racist treatment he endured. He protested when he was not allowed to stay in the same hotels or eat in the same restaurants as his teammates. His protests and growing popularity led to policy changes at some hotels and restaurants that allowed integration of blacks and whites.

When Robinson retired in 1957, he had become a hero in baseball. He had an impressive career batting average of .311. He also set a league record by stealing home base nineteen times over his career. In his first year of eligibility, Robinson was voted into the Hall of Fame. "Robinson could hit and bunt and steal and run," Roger Kahn wrote in *The Boys of Summer*. "He had intimidation skills, and he burned with a dark fire. He wanted passionately to win. He bore the burden of a pioneer and the weight made him stronger. If one can be certain of anything in baseball, it is that we shall not look upon his like again."[38]

Robinson's success in the major leagues opened the door for other black players, including Satchel Paige, Willie Mays, and Hank Aaron. In addition, Jackie Robinson's breaking baseball's color line struck a blow to segregation throughout society. Soon other racial barriers would fall.

Desegregation in Basketball

Following Robinson's historic entry into Major League Baseball, a number of African American athletes broke color barriers in other major sporting leagues. Before 1949 professional basketball teams ignored black athletes. As soon as Robinson made his debut in Major League Baseball, however, professional basketball teams sought black athletes as well.

Several black players recorded basketball firsts in 1950. Chuck Cooper of Duquesne University was the first black player to be drafted. Nat "Sweetwater" Clifton signed the first National Basketball Association (NBA) contract with the New York Knickerbockers. And because Earl Lloyd's team, the Washington Capitols, played a game before Clifton's debut with the Knickerbockers, Lloyd became the first to play in an NBA game. Before long, dozens of black athletes filled the rosters of professional basketball teams.

African Americans Join the NFL

Unlike baseball, which was already firmly segregated by the early twentieth century, a handful of black athletes played in the first professional football leagues in the 1920s. By 1933, however, white team owners had banded together to ban black players. Unable to play on National Football League (NFL) teams, black football players played on minor league teams or all-black barnstorming teams such as the Harlem Brown Bombers.

After the doors opened to African Americans in baseball, football's color line also cracked. In 1946 the NFL's Cleveland Rams moved to Los Angeles. Their stadium contract required that they

Harlem Globetrotters

Founded in 1926, the Harlem Globetrotters were one of the first all-black basketball teams. Although known today for their antics and trick shots, the Globetrotters were not always making people laugh on the court. The Globetrotters barnstormed around the country, playing close to one hundred games per year. Their talent led to an impressive record. In 1939 the Globetrotters played in the first national basketball championship, losing to the all-black New York Rens.

Because the Globetrotters could run up a high score on opposing teams, many teams did not want to play them. To encourage opposing teams to play, the Globetrotters experimented with adding comedy to their games. Trick plays and fancy ball handling helped to slow down the scoring and keep the crowds entertained.

When the National Basketball Association (NBA) began to integrate in the 1950s, opportunities for competitive games for barnstorming teams decreased. In response, the Globetrotters inttensified their focus on comedy. Ball gymnastics became their trademark style. Over the years, famous Globetrotters have included Reece "Goose" Tatum, Marques Haynes, Meadowlark Lemon, Wilt "the Stilt" Chamberlain, and Lynette Woodard, the first woman Globetrotter. The Globetrotters have entertained millions of fans in more than one hundred countries.

The Harlem Globetrotters team was formed in 1926. Known for their humorous antics on the court, the Globetrotters have been U.S. goodwill ambassadors to the world since the 1950s.

integrate their team. To comply, the Rams signed two black players, Woody Strode and Kenny Washington. The same year the Cleveland Browns, a member of the NFL rival All-American Football Conference, signed Marion Motley and Bill Willis.

Although signed in the same year, the four pioneer players had vastly different careers. Injuries ended Washington's career after three seasons, while Strode lasted just one season. In contrast, Willis and Motley enjoyed successful football careers and were inducted into the Pro Football Hall of Fame.

By 1949 three NFL teams had signed black players: the Rams, the Detroit Lions, and the New York Giants. By 1952 every team except the Washington Redskins had at least one black player on the team. A gradual desegregation of the major sports was under way.

The Civil Rights Movement Begins

While color lines were cracking in professional sports, the 1950s black community was becoming more vocal for change. Black papers and communities called for equal voting rights. They wanted access to the same public places as whites. Blacks wanted their children to have access to the same schools as whites. They also wanted the same job and housing opportunities as whites.

A major step toward civil rights occurred in 1953, when the Supreme Court ruled in *Terry v. Adams* that blacks be allowed to vote in primaries and all elections. The following year, on May 17, 1954, the Supreme Court issued a landmark decision in *Brown v. Board of Education of Topeka, Kansas*. In this decision the Court banned segregation of schools by race. This decision sent shockwaves across the country and angered southern whites. Tensions came to a head in Little Rock, Arkansas. When officials tried to integrate the school, they met resistance from white mobs and government officials. Images of the violence in Little Rock swept through newspapers and television. Eventually, President Dwight D. Eisenhower sent the Arkansas National Guard to Little Rock to take control and regain peace. Although Little Rock had calmed, the civil rights movement was just beginning.

Held to a Higher Standard

Surrounded by the country's racial turmoil, black athletes who broke the color barriers were cautioned by managers, owners, and

Fritz Pollard: Man of Firsts

One of football's fastest backs, Fritz Pollard was a trailblazer on the football field. In 1916 he became the first African American to play in the Rose Bowl as a member of Brown University's football team. The following year he led Brown in its first win against rival Harvard University. After graduation, Pollard joined the Akron Pros. He led the team to the first championship of the American Pro Football Association that year.

In 1921 Akron named him the first player-coach. He became the first and only African American to lead a professional football team, until Art Shell was named the head coach of the Oakland Raiders in 1989. Later Pollard signed with the Hammond Pros and changed positions. He became the first black quarterback in the game.

In 1921 Ohio's Akron Pros named Fritz Pollard as player-coach of the team. He was the first African American to lead a professional football team.

advisers to make sure their behavior on and off the field was spotless. While the white majority celebrated the individual athletic successes of men like Jesse Owens and Joe Louis, they still expected black athletes to observe society norms and "know their place." The sporting world expected athletes, especially black ones, to be humble and accommodating, not prideful and outspoken.

For the most part, black athletes during the 1940s and 1950s followed Robinson's example. Most were cautious not to step on social barriers while they broke sport's color barriers. According to historian John C. Walter, "The well-worn phrase was that these people knew that their behavior on field and off was to be a 'credit to their race.' These men, therefore, had to carry the burden of double circumspection, to play better than white players and also to conduct a life that was far more exemplary than both their white on-the-field counterparts and the ordinary white citizen."[39]

Chapter Four

An Uneven Progress

Although baseball, basketball, and football began integrating black athletes after World War II, other areas of sport did not immediately embrace integration. In particular, tennis and golf clung to their whites-only status for many more years.

United Golf Association

The game of golf originated in Scotland and was introduced to the United States in the 1880s. In golf's early days, black athletes were allowed to compete with whites. In fact, one of the earliest professional golfers was an African American named John Shippen Jr. In 1896 Shippen tied for fifth place in the U.S. Open Golf Tournament, one of golf's four major annual tournaments.

In 1916 the U.S. Golf Association, the governing body for golf, adopted a whites-only clause. Blacks could no longer play professional golf. Many golf courses also restricted access to blacks. In 1939 estimates show that of the more than five thousand golf facilities in the United States, less than twenty allowed black players to golf. As a result, many blacks learned golf as caddies, and golfers' assistants. It was one of the only ways they could play on private or public courses.

Golfer Robert Hawkins formed the United Golf Association (UGA) in 1926. The UGA was a professional league for black golfers. The UGA organized a series of tournaments for black golfers, playing on the few courses that allowed blacks. The UGA tour developed several black golfing stars, including Howard Wheeler, Eural Clark, Calvin Searles, Teddy Rhodes, and Bill Spiller. Women also played on the UGA tour. One of those women was tennis star Althea Gibson. She would eventually become the first black golfer accepted into the Ladies Professional Golf Association (LPGA) in 1963.

Sweet Swinger: Teddy Rhodes

One of the greatest black golfers of the 1940s was Teddy Rhodes. In the late 1940s and early 1950s, Rhodes dominated the UGA tour. He won the Joe Louis Invitational in Detroit four years in a row and the National Negro Open title three years in a row. He caught the attention of heavyweight boxing champion Louis, who hired Rhodes as his personal golf instructor. Because of Rhodes's graceful golf swing, Louis nicknamed him Sweet Swinger in 1945. He played in the 1948 U.S. Open, the second African American golfer to enter. He shot a 70 in the first round before he eventually faded behind winner Ben Hogan. "Teddy was a fantastic golfer," said Lee Elder, who in 1975 became the first African American to play in the prestigious Masters Golf Tournament. "His game was a carbon copy of Calvin Peete's, so straight that you could draw an arrow [with it]. His iron game was probably the best that I'll ever see."[40]

At the time, the Professional Golfers' Association (PGA) had a whites-only clause in its constitution. The rule stated that only whites could be PGA members and play in PGA tournaments. Black golfers like Rhodes knew about the PGA's whites-only clause. They also knew that three major tournaments were different: the Los Angeles Open, the Canadian Open, and the Tam O'Shanter World Championship of Golf in Chicago. These events allowed any qualified player to enter, regardless of race. In these events Rhodes could prove that he could swing with the world's best golfers.

In 1948 Rhodes saw his opportunity to break into PGA events. He entered the Los Angeles Open and finished a strong twentieth place. The PGA's tour rules stated that the top sixty golfers at the Los Angeles Open would automatically qualify to play in another

PGA tournament, the Richmond Open in California. The Richmond Open had traditionally been only accessible to whites. Now Rhodes and another black golfer, Bill Spiller, who had also qualified at the Los Angeles Open, headed to Richmond to play.

After finishing a practice round at Richmond Country Club, Spiller, Rhodes, and Madison Gunter, a local black amateur golfer, learned that they would not be allowed to play in the tournament. They were told it was because they were not members of the PGA. Yet Spiller and Rhodes could not join the PGA because the organization refused to accept black members.

Lawsuit Against the PGA

After the rejection Spiller contacted an attorney. He and Rhodes filed a $315,000 lawsuit against the Richmond Country Club and

Barred from competing in a Professional Golfers' Association (PGA) tournament because they were black, Bill Spiller, pictured, and Teddy Rhodes sued the PGA. The organization agreed to let blacks play— only to go back on its word once the lawsuit was dropped.

Charlie Sifford

Before Tiger Woods, Charlie Sifford paved the way for African American golfers. Born in Charlotte, North Carolina, in 1922, Sifford caddied as a young boy to earn money. He learned to love the game of golf. But in the 1930s a black man could not play on a Charlotte country club golf course. So in 1940 Sifford moved to Philadelphia, where he was allowed to play.

In 1947 Jackie Robinson broke the color line in Major League Baseball. His actions inspired Sifford, who told Robinson that he planned to play professional golf, although it was as white as baseball had been before Robinson. Between 1952 and 1956 Sifford won the national Negro Open five straight times. He pushed golf's color barrier, playing in some events organized by the white golf establishment, including the 1952 Phoenix Open.

Finally, in 1960 Sifford earned his PGA player card. A year later the Professional Golfers' Association (PGA) of America dropped its whites-only clause. Although Sifford had passed his golfing prime, he went on to win twice on the PGA tour. He also won the 1975 PGA Seniors' Championship. In 2004 Sifford became the first black golfer to be elected into the World Golf Hall of Fame. "If you try hard enough," Sifford said, "anything can happen."

Quoted in World Golf Hall of Fame. "World Golf Hall of Fame Profile: Charlie Sifford." www.worldgolfhalloffame. org/hof/memberphp?member=1105.

Charles Sifford earned his PGA card in 1960. Despite his advancing age, he won two tournaments on the PGA tour. Sifford was the first black golfer to be elected into the World Golf Hall of Fame.

the PGA of America. The suit claimed that Spiller and Rhodes were being denied their right to earn a living as professional golfers because of their race. It also claimed that the PGA was a closed shop, an establishment that prevented nonunion members from joining, which was illegal under the 1947 Taft-Hartley Act. A hearing was scheduled for September 1948. A few days before the hearing, the PGA offered to allow blacks to play in PGA tournaments if Spiller and Rhodes dropped the lawsuit.

The PGA, however, had no intention of letting black golfers play in its tournaments. After the men dropped the lawsuit, the organization quickly changed its tournament policy. Tournaments were no longer called "opens." Instead, they were "invitational" events. Individual tournaments and its sponsors invited players to participate. No black golfers received invitations.

Still resisting integration, the PGA banned boxing champ Louis from the San Diego Open in 1952. Louis, an avid amateur golfer with a single-digit handicap, had been invited by tournament sponsors to bring attention to the event. This time the PGA's decision to bar a world-famous athlete brought national attention to the discrimination in golf. Newspapers around the country picked up the story. By the end of the week, the PGA announced that while it would still not allow blacks to become members, it would no longer keep them from playing in events if they were invited and qualified.

Opening the Greens

After the 1952 San Diego Open, some tournaments did offer invitations to black golfers. A week after the San Diego Open, Rhodes and several other black golfers were invited to qualify in the Phoenix Open. Because most of the white pros refused to play with a black man, the black golfers were paired together. When they teed off on the first hole, they discovered that someone had filled the first hole's cup with human feces. Despite the distractions, Rhodes qualified with a par 71. He refused to let the incident at the first hole upset his game. "Teddy told me that to get angry was the equivalent of losing your game," says Maggie Hathaway, a former golf writer and editor for the black-owned weekly *Los Angeles Sentinel*. "Getting angry made him so nervous that sometimes he drew his putter back and couldn't bring it forward."[41]

Rhodes played wherever he could for the rest of the 1950s. He eventually made it into sixty-nine PGA events, where he finished in the top twenty a total of nine times. In 1957 he won the National Negro Open title again. He also became a mentor and coach for future black golfing stars Elder and Gibson.

When the PGA finally eliminated its whites-only clause in 1961, it was too late for Rhodes. Suffering from a kidney ailment, he was unable to play at his former level. He died in 1969 from a heart attack. On November 14, 2009, the PGA of America bestowed posthumous membership upon Rhodes, Shippen, and Spiller. "If not for the mere color of their skin, these gentlemen would have most certainly become PGA members in their time," said past PGA president Jim Remy. "While we can never erase the past, we can do everything possible to advance the promise of diversity and hope for all."[42]

Serving on the Tennis Court

Like golf, tennis was resistant to integrating African American players into mainstream events. The game of tennis came to the United States in the 1870s. By 1890 African Americans were playing tennis. Yet in the early twentieth century, the United States Lawn Tennis Association (USLTA) did not admit African Americans to the majority of its events. As a result, a group of black tennis enthusiasts formed the American Tennis Association (ATA) in 1916. It became the first black sports organization in the United States.

Denied at USLTA events, the ATA developed its own tennis circuit. The organization held its first ATA National Championships at Baltimore's Druid Hill Park in August 1917. Because blacks were denied lodging at most hotels, the ATA held many of its early events at various black colleges, including Hampton Institute in Virginia, Morehouse College in Atlanta, Central State in Ohio, and Lincoln University in Pennsylvania. These campuses provided housing and tennis courts. Soon the ATA national championship became a highly anticipated social event for the black community. During the week of the tournament, enthusiasts planned dances, fashion shows, and other activities.

The color barrier in tennis began to crack in 1940 when the first interracial match was played. Don Budge, winner of the 1938 tennis Grand Slam, met ATA champion Jimmie McDaniel

In an exhibition in 1938, tennis player Jimmie McDaniel played white tennis star Don Budge. Despite the interracial pairing, match tennis would remain segregated until the 1950s.

in an exhibition match. Although Budge defeated McDaniel, he complimented the ATA champ. "Jimmy is a very good player, I'd say he'd rank with the first 10 of our white players,"[43] Budge said. Despite the match, tennis would remain mostly segregated until a young woman named Althea Gibson captured the nation's attention in 1950.

Althea Gibson

Born in 1927, Gibson moved with her family from South Carolina to Harlem, New York, as a toddler. As a child she loved to play sports. "I just wanted to play, play, play,"[44] she said. At first Gibson excelled at paddle tennis, a game similar to tennis that is played with a rubber ball and a paddle on a small court. She developed a reputation for crushing her opponents. Her play drew the attention of bandleader Buddy Walker. He thought court tennis might be a better challenge for the hard-hitting Gibson. Immediately, she connected with the game. Her intense play earned

After winning the Wimbledon and U.S. Open tournaments in 1957, Althea Gibson became the first black woman to receive the Female Athlete of the Year Award from Associated Press. She is considered the "Jackie Robinson of tennis" for breaking the color barrier in her sport.

Lucy Diggs Slowe

Considered by many to be the mother of black tennis, Lucy Diggs Slowe and other black athletes helped form the American Tennis Association (ATA) in 1916. She became the first African American woman to win a national championship in any sport when she won the women's singles title at the first ATA National Championship in 1917.

Off the court, Slowe was a champion for women and education. She was one of the founders and the first president of the Alpha Kappa Alpha sorority, the first sorority for African American women, at Howard University. After college, Slowe taught in the public school system. She became the first College Dean of Women at Howard University in 1922. She also was president of the National Association of College Women and the National Association of Women's Deans and Advisors of Girls in Colored Schools.

her a spot at the Cosmopolitan Tennis Club in Harlem. The club was home to elite black tennis players. Amazed by Gibson's power and skill, club members sponsored her junior club membership. Within a year Gibson's training paid off and she won the ATA's junior championship.

In 1946 Gibson's play attracted the attention of two southern doctors, Hubert Eaton and Robert Johnson, who were active in the black tennis community. They recognized her talent but knew that she needed training on and off the court. The doctors took Gibson under their wing and became her patrons. With the permission of her parents, they took her into their homes. Gibson lived with Eaton's family during the school year. During the summer she lived with the Johnsons. Under Eaton and Johnson's mentoring and connections, Gibson had access to top-notch instruction and competitions. She graduated from high school and attended Florida A&M on a tennis and basketball scholarship.

By age twenty Gibson had won ten consecutive ATA national championships. Despite her talent, the USLTA refused at first to let her compete with white players in the 1950 U.S. Nationals. Then Alice Marble, four-time winner of the event, wrote a scathing commentary in the July 1950 issue of *American Lawn*

Tennis magazine. "If Althea Gibson represents a challenge to the present crop of players, then it's only fair that they meet this challenge on the courts,"[45] Marble wrote. The USLTA eventually relented and allowed the Orange Law Tennis Club in South Orange, New Jersey, to invite Gibson to the 1950 Eastern Grass Court championships. Gibson did not win, but she earned a bid to the U.S. Nationals at Forest Hills in Queens, New York. At her debut at the 1950 U.S. Nationals, Gibson advanced to a historic match against the Wimbledon singles champion, Louise Brough. Although Gibson lost, she proved that she could play with the best. The next year, the USLTA invited her to play at Wimbledon.

Gibson won her first major tennis tournament at the 1956 French Open. In 1957 she won her first Wimbledon title. Recalling her preparation for the tournament, Gibson said, "I was ruthless on the tennis court. Win at any cost, I became an attacker. If your first serve ain't good, I'll knock it down your throat."[46] She also won the U.S. Nationals in the same year. During her career, Gibson won five Grand Slam singles titles and six doubles titles.

Yet even though Gibson had broken into formerly white tennis tournaments, she still experienced difficulties because of her color. Sometimes hotels denied her a room. At one time a hotel refused to book a reservation for a luncheon in her honor.

In recognition of her accomplishments, the Associated Press voted Gibson the Female Athlete of the Year in 1957. She was the first black woman to receive the honor. In 1958, during what may have been the peak of her tennis career, Gibson retired.

After tennis Gibson dabbled in singing, acting, and golf. In golf she became the first African American player on the LPGA tour and was ranked third in 1967. Yet Gibson will always be remembered as the tennis pioneer who paved the way for future African American tennis greats. Many call Gibson the "Jackie Robinson of tennis." Billie Jean King, winner of twelve Grand Slam singles titles, said, "If it hadn't been for her, it wouldn't have been so easy for Arthur (Ashe) or the ones who followed."[47]

Arthur Ashe

Despite Gibson's accomplishments, it was almost a decade before another African American tennis player rose to the top. On the men's side, a player named Arthur Ashe changed the history of

As a black tennis star, Arthur Ashe used his status to speak out in protest against South Africa's racist apartheid system and worked to end it. In 1973 he was finally granted a visa to play there and became the first African American to win a tournament in South Africa.

tennis with his skill and determination. Born in 1943 Ashe was an unlikely athletic star. As a child he was a shy, uncoordinated bookworm. "I was too small for any sport but tennis," he said. "I learned to swim when I was very young, but I was always a bit afraid of water. My father wouldn't let me play football because of my size."[48]

Ashe learned to play tennis in Richmond, Virginia's Brookfield Park. There he attracted the attention of Ronald Charity, a tennis player and coach. Charity was impressed with the young man's determination. He arranged for him to meet with Robert Johnson, who years earlier had coached and mentored tennis champion Gibson. In 1953 Johnson took Ashe to his home for the summer. He tutored young black men and women, including Ashe, and helped them earn tennis college scholarships. With Johnson's coaching, Ashe's game grew stronger.

In 1955 Ashe won his first tournament, a twelve-and-under singles event. Three years later he was the first African American to play in the Maryland Boys championship. As he won boys' and men's ATA titles in the late 1950s and early 1960s, people began to notice Ashe. In 1965 Ashe leaped onto the national stage when he won the National Collegiate Athletic Association (NCAA) title while a student at the University of California–Los Angeles (UCLA). While winning on the court, Ashe still experienced the sting of discrimination. In college he was once asked to sit out of a tournament because black players were not allowed to enter.

In 1968 Ashe won the U.S. Open. Later that year he was the first African American to be invited to play on the U.S. Davis Cup team. Ashe won thirty-five amateur singles titles. As a professional he triumphed with thirty-three singles titles, including the 1970 Australian Open and Wimbledon in 1975.

Ashe Speaks for Change

Ashe used his status as a black tennis star in a game dominated by white players to speak out about causes he supported. He pushed to create inner-city tennis programs for underprivileged kids. He helped found the Association of Tennis Professionals. In addition, he frequently protested the practice of apartheid in South Africa.

Although Ashe had become a world-renown tennis star, the South African government denied him a visa to play in the 1969

Wilma Rudolph: Born to Run

At the 1960 Olympics in Rome, Wilma Rudolph became the fastest woman in the world. Spectators were cautioned not to blink during one of Rudolph's races. If they did they might miss her. At the Games, Rudolph became the first American woman to win three gold medals in one Olympics, the 100-meter, 200-meter, and 4x100-meter relay. This feat was even more spectacular for a woman whose doctors once called crippled.

Born prematurely in 1940, Rudolph spent much of her childhood in bed. She contracted polio, which can cause paralysis, and was fitted with metal leg braces at age six. Rudolph was determined to regain her ability to walk. She snuck out of her braces whenever she had a chance. Her brothers and sisters took turns massaging her legs, and her mother took her for weekly therapy sessions. By age nine she was out of her braces and playing basketball. In high school she became an all-state player, scoring a state record of forty-nine points in one game.

When Ed Temple, the Tennessee State University track coach, asked Rudolph's basketball coach to form a track team, Wilma Rudolph found her calling. "I don't know why I run so fast. I just run," she said.

Quoted in M.B. Roberts. "Rudolph Ran and World Went Wild." ESPN.com.http://espn.go.com/sportscentury/features/00016444.html.

Born prematurely, Wilma Rudolph spent much of her early childhood bedridden. Nevertheless, at the 1960 Olympic Games in Rome, she became the first American woman to win three gold medals at one Olympics.

South African Open. Ashe petitioned the International Lawn Tennis Federation to expel South Africa from its membership. In 1973 Ashe finally received a visa to play in South Africa. He became the first black player to win a title in the country, a doubles championship. "You have shown our black youth that they can compete with whites and win,"[49] said African poet Don Mattera.

Ashe's tennis career ended prematurely when he suffered a heart attack in 1979. He retired in 1980 with thirty-three singles titles and 818 career wins. In 1992 Ashe announced that he had contracted AIDS from a blood transfusion. He died in 1993. Ashe was one of the most notable tennis players of his time. He may be remembered more, however, for the causes he championed both on and off the tennis court.

Chapter Five

The Civil Rights Era: Athletes Speak for Change

In the 1960s the African American community challenged racial injustice with intensity and determination. Previously, athletes had been cautioned against speaking out on racial issues. Now three pioneer athletes, basketball player Bill Russell, football star Jim Brown, and boxer Cassius Clay, who would change his name to Muhammad Ali, used their status as sports superstars to speak out for civil rights. Their actions inspired athletes and citizens alike to stay strong and united in the quest for equality. They would leave a lasting legacy on sport and society.

Bill Russell

In the late 1950s and 1960s, one of the greatest basketball defenders in league history was Boston Celtic center Bill Russell. He led his team to an amazing eleven titles in thirteen seasons. In a league known its for runaway offense, Russell's aggressive defensive style revolutionized how basketball was played. He swooped across the court, blocked shots, and rebounded balls. His career average of 22.5 rebounds per game stands as the second highest of all time. "I was an innovator," Russell said. "I started blocking shots although I had never seen a shot blocked before that."[50] He could leave his man and slide over to defend against another opponent driving toward the basket. Other centers copied Russell's style of play, although most were not as skilled.

Despite his individual greatness, many considered Russell a master at making the players around him play better. Hall of Famer Tom Heinsohn, Russell's Celtics teammate, said, "He was such a great competitor, and that will always define Bill Russell.

Bill Russell, seen making a power shot, led the Boston Celtics to eleven National Basketball Association (NBA) titles in thirteen seasons. He is considered one of the greatest of the "big men" in NBA history.

We had a lot of parts on our team—[Bob] Cousy was the ball handler, I was the scorer, I could always get a shot off—but Russell was the one who held it all together. It all started with him."[51]

Born William Fenton Russell in 1934 in Louisiana, Russell moved with his family to California as a child. Daily he watched his father and mother experience discrimination. As a teen Russell grew to be more than 6 feet tall. Despite his height, he showed little athletic skill on the basketball court. In fact, his junior high school team cut him. In high school the coach decided to take a chance on Russell. "I believe that man saved me from becoming a juvenile delinquent," wrote Russell in his first autobiography, *Go Up for Glory*. "If I hadn't had basketball, all my energies and frustrations would surely have been carried in some other direction."[52] Russell did not play as a starter until his senior year. When he did play, his unique style of jumping to block shots had never been seen before.

Only one college offered Russell a basketball scholarship—the University of San Francisco (USF). African American players were still rare in college basketball. Russell's USF team became the first to have three black players as starters. In college Russell exploded on the court and became a dominating center. While he played, USF won two consecutive National Collegiate Athletic Association (NCAA) championships and had a string of sixty consecutive wins.

During his time with USF, Russell faced the reality of discrimination against black players. Crowds yelled insults at him and his black teammates. During the 1955 All-College tournament in Oklahoma City, one hotel refused to allow Russell and his black teammates to book a room. In protest, the entire USF team chose to stay instead in an empty college dormitory.

Red Auerbach, the coach of the Boston Celtics, noticed Russell's play as a college player. He thought that Russell's defensive skills were just what the Celtics needed to win a championship. He selected Russell in the 1956 National Basketball Association (NBA) draft. Before Russell joined the Celtics, he won a gold medal with the 1956 U.S. Olympic basketball team in Melbourne, Australia. Then Russell joined the Celtics in the middle of the 1956–1957 season.

Russell dominated on the court, blocking shots and quickly leading the league in average rebounds per game. With his presence on the court, the Celtics began to win. Russell's Celtics won their first NBA championship in 1957. Over the next thirteen years, they would win an incredible eleven titles, including an unmatched streak of eight consecutive championships. During that time, Russell was named NBA's Most Valuable Player five times.

Even when the Celtics were at their peak, Russell struggled against discrimination. There were many empty seats in the Boston Garden where the Celtics played, while less successful teams sold out their arenas. Some white Boston sportswriters refused to vote for him as the most valuable player because he was black. When Russell bought a house in a white Boston suburb, neighbors harassed and threatened him. One time vandals broke into his home and marked the walls with graffiti.

The Civil Rights Act of 1964

Signed into law on July 2, 1964, the Civil Rights Act of 1964 outlawed major forms of discrimination against blacks and women in the United States. The act outlawed racial segregation in schools, at work, and in public facilities. It also ended unequal application of voter registration requirements.

President Lyndon B. Johnson signed the bill into law in a nationwide television broadcast. Before signing, he said:

> We believe that all men are created equal—yet many are denied equal treatment. We believe that all men have certain inalienable rights. We believe that all men are entitled to the blessings of liberty —yet millions are being deprived of those blessings, not because of their own failures, but because of the color of their skin. The reasons are deeply embedded in history and tradition and the nature of man. We can understand without rancor or hatred how all this happens. But it cannot continue. Our Constitution, the foundation of our Republic, forbids it. The principles of our freedom forbid it. Morality forbids it. And the law I sign tonight forbids it.

Quoted in CongressLink. "Major Features of the Civil Rights Act of 1964." www.congresslink.org/print_basics_histmats_civilrights64text.htm.

In spite of the threats, Russell was determined to use his public spotlight to support the civil rights movement. Even though he knew it would damage his popularity with white fans, he joined civil rights activist and minister Martin Luther King Jr. in the 1963 March on Washington. He also vocally supported boxer Ali when Ali protested the Vietnam War.

When Celtics coach Auerbach moved to the team's front office in 1966, the team named Russell as his replacement. Still playing, Russell became the first black coach for a major professional sports team in the United States. At a press conference announcing his new job, Russell remembers a reporter asking if he could coach the white players without being prejudiced. "Now, I didn't recall anybody asking a white coach if he could coach the black guys without being prejudiced. All I said was, 'Yeah,'"[53] Russell said.

In the spring of 1968, King was assassinated. Many African Americans were upset by the violent death of the peaceful leader. Russell vocally supported the rights of African Americans to defend themselves against racial violence. He did not care how that affected his public image. Instead, Russell remained steadfast in his convictions.

After winning his eleventh championship in the 1969 finals, Russell retired from the Celtics. In 1972 the Celtics retired Russell's jersey, and in 1975 Russell was inducted into the Basketball Hall of Fame. However, he decided not to attend either event. Instead, he issued a short statement saying that he preferred not to be inducted. Years later Russell explained his position, saying he did not want to be associated with certain members of the Hall of Fame, in particular Adolph Rupp. Rupp was a coach at the University of Kentucky and was a well-known racist and supporter of segregated sports. "I did not want to be associated with him or anyone else of his racial views. I saw that as my free choice to make,"[54] Russell wrote. As a result of his decision to shun induction, many people harshly criticized Russell. Yet he demonstrated once again his willingness to stand up for his beliefs no matter what others said about him.

Since his retirement, Russell has been an active voice for civil rights and diversity. He has partnered with the NBA and the U.S. government to hold basketball clinics in more than fifty countries on six continents. He also was the first winner of the NBA's Civil

Off the court, basketball star Bill Russell was an outspoken advocate for civil rights. In 2011 President Barack Obama awarded Russell the nation's highest civilian honor—the Presidential Medal of Freedom.

Rights Award. In 2011 President Barack Obama awarded Russell the Presidential Medal of Freedom, the nation's highest civilian honor.

Jim Brown

For many Jim Brown was the greatest running back of all time. During his nine-year career with the Cleveland Browns, he did more than run; he caught passes, returned kickoffs, and even threw touchdown passes. Over his career Brown accumulated 12,312 rushing yards and 15,459 combined net yards. He played in nine Pro Bowls, one in each year of his career. He also earned the NFL's Most Valuable Player Award four times.

As a teenager Brown lived in Manhasset, New York, a wealthy community where his mother worked as a domestic. He attended Manhasset High School and became an athletic standout. During his high school years, Brown was mentored by a group of white professional men who encouraged him to study and run for student government.

When Brown attended Syracuse University in Upstate New York, it was an eye-opening experience for him. He was the only African American player on the football team. At Syracuse Brown encountered more problems with discrimination than he had in high school. "I met all those loving white people at Manhasset. Then I went to Syracuse, ran chin first into overt racism. Someone had changed all the rules, and forgotten to tell me,"[55] he said.

Troubled, Brown said he realized that he was not being judged as an individual. Instead, he was being defined by his race. Many people warned Brown against acting too much like a former Syracuse black football player who had dared to date white coeds at a time when mixed-race dating was frowned upon. Brown recalls:

> I came up at the crossroads of segregation. There were still colleges where black players couldn't play. There were teams that would go south, and black players had to stay in private homes. It was a blessing [as a black man to be able to play college football] because there were opportunities, but it was demeaning because you were looked on as inferior. It was almost as if you'd been given a favor. And you always felt you had to perform much, much better.[56]

Many think Jim Brown is the greatest running back of all time.
During his nine-year career he gained 12,312 rushing yards and
15,459 total yards. His 5.7 yards per carry is still an NFL record.

At Syracuse Brown quickly became a star in four sports and earned All-American honors. In 1957 the NFL's Cleveland Browns selected Brown as their number one draft pick. With his strength, speed, and agility, he quickly became the premier running back in the league. Brown said:

> But you could never just play and not be cognizant of the social situation in the country. Every day of your life, that was in your mind. You had to question why they put black players only at certain positions, why there were positions that blacks weren't smart enough to play. So I was very conscious of the civil rights movement and very active in what I call the movement for dignity, equality and justice. In fact, it superseded my interest in sports. Sports gave me an opportunity to help the cause.[57]

Brown used his star status to speak out about racism in sports and society. "I doubt that the American white man realizes that the time has come when he must make a move," Brown wrote. "He must give us the laws that make us free men and he must enforce those laws. . . . I am not interested in winning freedom for my three children . . . the white man lives today. I, too, intend to live today."[58] Although he made many people uncomfortable, others respected Brown's honesty. "Please keep talking," wrote one St. Louis man. "Even though your words hurt, they may open some eyes and change some actions while there's time."[59]

Brown shocked football fans when he retired in 1966 at the peak of his career. He left football as the NFL's all-time leading rusher. After his retirement Brown pursued a movie career and mentored athletes. He also works in the community to help rehabilitate gang members and prisoners.

Muhammad Ali

On February 26, 1964, a boxer named Cassius Clay became the youngest heavyweight champion of the world. "I am the greatest,"[60] Clay shouted after he defeated Sonny Liston. Shortly after winning, Clay stunned the world when he announced that he was a member of the Nation of Islam. Also known as the Black Muslims, the Nation of Islam is a militant religious group that supported violent civil rights protests and separation of the races. By announcing his allegiance to the group, the popular boxer immediately became one of the country's most controversial figures. He also changed his name; he would now be known as Muhammad Ali.

Born in 1942 in Kentucky, Cassius Marcellus Clay Jr. started boxing around the age of twelve. By the time he was sixteen, Clay won the Louisville Golden Gloves light heavyweight title. After high school, Clay won his second National Amateur Athletic Union title and traveled to Rome, Italy, to represent the United States in the 1960 Olympic Games. In Rome Clay won the gold medal.

Back at home Clay hired a trainer and began fighting professionally. A showman, Clay announced before each fight which round he would win. Amazingly, his predictions often came true. His entertaining style attracted growing audiences. He was undefeated after nineteen professional fights, winning fifteen of them by knockout. Finally, in 1964 he got his chance at the heavyweight title with a match against reigning champ Sonny Liston.

Before the fight, most boxing experts did not give the twenty-two-year-old Clay a chance against the more experienced Liston. One of Clay's advisers told him to "float like a butterfly, sting like a bee," a phrase that will always be associated with Clay. Clay's quick feet and stinging fists proved to be too much for the slower Liston. Clay won in six rounds.

The next day Clay announced his affiliation with the Nation of Islam and his name change. Many people were confused and angry that their sports hero was now supporting a group that shunned Christianity and openly criticized whites.

Even black Americans were disturbed by Clay's announcement. Christianity had been a strong pillar of faith in the black community for decades. Many did not support Clay's decision to leave Christianity. Despite the disagreement over his religious choice, however, many black Americans respected Clay for standing up for his beliefs.

In 1966 the U.S. military drafted Ali during the Vietnam War. Ali, along with other members of the Nation of Islam, did not support the war. He requested to be excused from military duty because of his religious beliefs. The U.S. government denied the request and ordered him to be inducted into the military. Ali refused and issued a statement saying, "I have searched my conscience and I find I cannot be true to my belief in my religion by accepting such a call."[61]

On February 25, 1964, a young Cassius Clay, left, pummels heavyweight champion Sonny Liston to become the youngest heavyweight champion of the world.

Ali's stand had far-reaching consequences. Immediately, boxing organizations stripped the champ of his heavyweight crown and revoked his boxing license. The U.S. government indicted him and found him guilty of draft evasion in 1967. He was fined ten thousand dollars and sentenced to five years in prison. Ali appealed the ruling. In 1971 the U.S. Supreme Court overturned the conviction. It ruled that Ali's objection to the war was based on legitimate religious beliefs. Four years after being banned from boxing, Ali was free to resume his career.

Returning to the boxing ring, Ali won his first fight. He challenged undefeated Joe Frazier in the "Fight of the Century" in 1971. The match lasted fifteen rounds before Frazier knocked out Ali. It was Ali's first professional loss. In 1974 Ali would win a rematch against Frazier. Also in 1974, Ali regained his heavyweight crown by beating reigning champ George Foreman in the "Rumble in the Jungle," a match staged in Zaire (today's Democratic Republic of the Congo) In 1975 Ali battled Frazier for a third time, this time in a matchup dubbed the "Thrilla in Manila." Held in the Philippines, it is considered by many to be the greatest boxing match of all time. Ali won again. By the late 1970s, Ali's career began to decline, and he lost several bouts. He retired from boxing in 1981.

In 1984 Ali announced that he had Parkinson's disease, a degenerative neurological disorder. Over the years, the disease would rob him of the graceful movements he showed in the boxing ring. Despite his health challenges, Ali has spent much of his time supporting charitable causes. He has traveled to many countries to help those less fortunate. In 1998 he was chosen to be a United Nations Messenger of Peace because of his work. In addition, in 2005 Ali received the Presidential Medal of Freedom from President George W. Bush.

Throughout his career, Ali was known as a fighter, both in and out of the ring. People either loved or hated him. Yet his willingness to stand up for his beliefs, even at the expense of his own career, won him respect.

Civil Rights Movement

While Russell, Brown, and Ali made headlines, the civil rights movement picked up momentum. In the late 1950s and early 1960s, members of the black community grew impatient. They were tired of waiting for the government to act on civil rights issues and decided to take matters into their own hands. They organized sit-ins and protests to push for integration of public places like lunch counters, beaches, and libraries. At first the demonstrations were peaceful. As they spread throughout the South, however, protesters faced insults, bomb threats, and physical violence.

The "Say Hey Kid": Willie Mays

Considered by many to be the best player in baseball history, Willie Mays, known as the "Say Hey Kid," did it all. He could hit almost any pitch, becoming the first player in the majors to hit three hundred home runs. He ranks fourth in career home runs, behind Babe Ruth, Hank Aaron, and Barry Bonds. He was the first to steal three hundred bases. His fielding and throwing are legendary. In the 1954 World Series, Mays made an amazing catch of the Cleveland Indian Vic Wertz's deep ball and rocketed an infield throw that kept the Indians from scoring.

Mays's career began in the Negro leagues in 1948. In 1950 he was signed by the New York Giants. After a two-year stint in the army, Mays played for the Giants for more than a decade, winning the World Series in

1954. He recorded a career batting average of .302. He won the Golden Glove Award twelve times and was voted the National League's Most Valuable Player twice. In 1966 the Giants signed Mays to a new contract, making him the highest-paid player in baseball history. In recognition of his great career, Mays was inducted into baseball's Hall of Fame in 1979.

The "Say Hey Kid," Willie Mays, began his career in 1948 in the Negro leagues and by 1950 had signed with the New York Giants. Mays, who had a lifetime batting average of .302 and twelve Gold Glove Awards, was inducted into the Baseball Hall of Fame in 1979.

U.S. athletes Tommie Smith, center, and John Carlos, right, give the black power salute on the medal podium at the 1968 Mexico City Olympic Games. For their actions, they were stripped of their medals.

1968 Olympic Boycott

In this environment black athletes were more empowered than ever to use their status as sports figures to call attention to civil rights causes. In 1968 the Olympic Games were scheduled to be held in Mexico. To the outrage of many people around the world, South Africa supported the practice of apartheid, a government policy of racial segregation and political and economic discrimination against blacks. Nevertheless, the International Olympic Committee (IOC) planned to allow South African athletes to participate in the Games.

In protest of this decision, Harry Edwards, a sociology professor at San Diego State University, called for African American athletes to boycott the 1968 Olympic Games. Star athletes Russell, Brown, and Ali publicly supported the plan. Their star power brought more attention to the proposed boycott. Eventually more than thirty countries joined the call for a boycott. This got the IOC's attention, and it banned South Africa from the Games. With this decision, African American athletes decided to compete in the Games.

Olympic Protest

Although black athletes joined the 1968 Olympics, some used the international stage for individual protest. In the 200-meter race, sprinters Tommie Smith and John Carlos won the gold and bronze medals, respectively. When they arrived at the medal ceremony, Smith and Carlos wore black socks and no shoes to symbolize African American poverty. They each wore a black glove to represent African American strength and unity. Smith wore a scarf and Carlos wore beads, in remembrance of lynching victims. As they stood on the medal podium during the playing of the U.S. national anthem, the two men bowed their heads and raised a clenched fist. This image was broadcast to an international television audience. "It was a polarizing moment because it was seen as an example of black power radicalism," said Doug Hartmann, a University of Minnesota sociologist. "Mainstream America hated what they did."[62]

Olympic officials swiftly reacted to the athletes' protest. They banned Smith and Carlos from the Games. The men returned to the United States, where reaction to their action was mixed. Democratic vice presidential nominee Edmund Muskie told the

The Home Run King: Hank Aaron

Known for years as baseball's home run king, Henry "Hank" Aaron played for twenty-three years. He holds many of baseball's most revered records, including runs batted in, extra base hits, and most years with thirty or more home runs. He also held the record for most career home runs (755) until Barry Bonds broke it in 2007.

As a young player, Aaron noticed that he made more money when he hit home runs. Over the rest of his career, Aaron cracked a steady stream of thirty to forty home run seasons. In 1973 Aaron finished the season one home run short of Babe Ruth's record of 714.

On the brink of breaking Ruth's record, Aaron faced a surge of criticism. As many as three thousand letters a day arrived at the Braves' offices for Aaron. While some fans congratulated him, many were upset that a black man was going to break Ruth's record. Some letters contained death threats. Aaron did not let it stop him. He tied Ruth's record on opening day in 1974. Then on April 15 he cracked his record 715th home run. More than fifty thousand fans cheered as he circled the bases, the new home run king.

In April 1974 Hank Aaron watches his 715th home run fly into baseball history as he breaks Babe Ruth's career home run record.

press that the men probably should not have made the black power statement at the Olympics. But baseball great Jackie Robinson criticized the U.S. Olympic Committee for banning Smith and Carlos. "The Olympic Committee made a grave mistake in suspending them. I take pride in their proudness in being black. What they did had nothing to do with shaming this country,"[63] he said. Regardless of public opinion, the moment became one of the most enduring symbols of athletes and the civil rights movement.

Chapter Six

Rising to the Top

In the years following the tumultuous civil rights era, African American athletes have excelled in professional and college sports. The numbers of black athletes in professional leagues has increased significantly. Incomes have also risen dramatically, with African American athletes becoming some of the highest paid in sports. In addition, a significant number of African American athletes have received lucrative endorsement contracts for products ranging from breakfast cereals to automobiles. Only fifty years earlier, the idea of an African American athlete on the cover of a cereal box would have been unthinkable.

Taking the Field

In the years since the 1970s, college and professional sports have increasingly become more integrated. According to a 2010 report by the Institute for Diversity and Ethics in Sport at the University of Central Florida, African Americans represent 45.8 percent of Division I football and 60.9 percent of basketball athletes. In addition, college football's most coveted individual honor, the Heisman Trophy, has been awarded to several African American players in recent years. In 2010 Cam Newton, an African American quarterback from Auburn University, won the award.

In the major professional leagues, more African American athletes are taking the field. According to the Institute for Diversity and Ethics in Sport, African American athletes were 67 percent of National Football League (NFL) players in 2009. In the National Basketball Association (NBA) 77 percent of players were African American. In Major League Baseball (MLB) 38.3 percent of players were people of color at the 2011 season start. With more opportunities to play, several African American athletes have risen to the top of their sport. They have become true American superstars.

Golfing Great: Tiger Woods

In 2010 golfer Tiger Woods topped *Sports Illustrated's* list of top-earning athletes. He made $62.3 million from endorsements, salary, and winnings in 2010. Although his image took a hit in 2009 for off-the-course activities, Woods was the definition of excellence in sport.

Born Eldrick Tont Woods in 1975 to an African American father and Thai mother, "Tiger" Woods began playing golf as a child. By age eight, he was showing off his skills on morning television shows. Woods won a number of U.S. amateur golf titles before turning professional in 1996. At the age of twenty-one, Woods won one of golf's most legendary tournaments, the Masters, in 1997. He became the youngest golfer and first African American to win the Masters. He destroyed the competition, posting a record score of 270 and beating the next closest opponent by twelve strokes.

Over the next decade Woods dominated the field. Through the beginning of 2011, Woods won ninety-five tournaments, seventy-one of them on the Professional Golfer's Association (PGA) tour. He has won fourteen of golf's "major" tournaments, putting him only four wins behind legendary golfer Jack Nicklaus's long-standing record of eighteen major victories. When Woods earned his second Masters victory in 2001, he became the first golfer in history to hold the current title on all four professional major championships.

Not only did Woods win tournaments, he became legendary for the ways that he won. He holds or shares the record for low score in three of golf's four major championships (in golf, the lower the score, the better). His victories on golf's most prestigious stages, the U.S. Open and the Masters, came by record margins, blowing away the competition by fifteen and twelve strokes,

Tiger Woods holds the Masters trophy and wears the coveted green jacket of a Masters Tournament winner. In 1997 Woods became the youngest man and first African American to win the Masters.

respectively. "Tiger Woods is, without a doubt, the greatest athlete of this generation . . . he sets a new standard for generations of athletes, in every sport, to follow,"[64] wrote sportscaster Ed Berliner in 2009.

Venus and Serena Williams

The Williams sisters took the tennis world by storm in the 1990s. Known for their powerful ground strokes and booming serves, Venus and Serena Williams quickly rose to the top of the women's tennis rankings. The sisters brought a new power and athleticism to women's tennis.

The sisters' father, Richard Williams, loved the game of tennis. He dreamed that one of his daughters would play the sport. When Venus and Serena showed talent, he practiced and coached them from a young age. By age ten, the sisters were winning tournaments. A few years later they turned professional.

In 1999 Serena defeated defending champ Martina Hingis to win the U.S. Open, her first tennis Grand Slam title. The following year Venus won two Grand Slam events, Wimbledon and the U.S. Open. She became the first black woman to hold both titles since Althea Gibson won them in 1958. At the 2000 Olympics Venus won the women's tennis gold medal, and the pair won the doubles gold.

Venus repeated as champion at Wimbledon and the U.S. Open in 2001, beating Serena in the U.S. Open finals. In 2002 Serena beat Venus in the finals of three Grand Slam events: the French Open, Wimbledon, and the U.S. Open. Her victories launched Serena to the number one ranking in women's tennis. She became

The Williams sisters, Serena, left, and Venus, took the tennis world by storm in 1999. By 2011 Serena had won thirteen Grand Slam singles titles and Venus nine. Together they won an Olympic gold medal in doubles play in 2000.

the first African American woman to end the tennis year ranked first since Gibson in 1958.

The sisters' talent has led to many more titles. As of the beginning of the 2011 season, Serena had won thirteen Grand Slam singles titles, and Venus had won nine Grand Slam events. In addition, the duo has recorded numerous tour wins, doubles championships, and another doubles gold medal in the 2008 Olympics. Their success on the court has also led to lucrative endorsement contracts. In 2004 *Forbes* magazine ranked the sisters as the world's highest-paid female athletes.

Venus and Serena recognize that their success could not have come without African American athletes who blazed the trail before them. "I am grateful to Althea Gibson for having the strength and courage to break through the racial barriers in tennis. Her accomplishments set the stage for my success, and through players like myself, Serena, and many others to come, her legacy will live on,"[65] said Venus at Gibson's death in 2002.

Be Like Mike: Michael Jordan

Considered by many to be the best basketball player in history, Michael Jordan dominated the NBA from the mid-1980s through the late 1990s. With his gravity-defying slam dunks and acrobatic moves, Jordan led the Chicago Bulls to six national championships. He also accumulated ten scoring titles, fourteen All-Star Game appearances, and five NBA Most Valuable Player awards. "Michael Jordan is the greatest basketball player of all time," said former Phoenix Suns coach Paul Westphal. "He's the greatest point guard ever. He's the greatest shooting guard ever. He's the greatest small forward ever. He'd probably rank in the top five among power forwards and centers. I don't think Michael Jordan could guard Michael Jordan."[66]

Jordan's spectacular play revived waning interest in the NBA. His smooth, bald head, charming smile, and hardworking attitude made him likeable. It also helped him become one of the greatest sports marketing success stories in history. When Jordan was an NBA rookie, sports apparel companies paid athletes to endorse and wear their products. In 1984 no one believed that a black athlete could successfully be the centerpiece of a marketing campaign. "It was heresy to believe that Michael Jordan could

Michael Jordan, with the ball, is considered by many to be the best basketball player in history. Jordan won five NBA Most Valuable Player awards, ten scoring titles, and had fourteen All-Star Game appearances. He also led the Chicago Bulls to six NBA titles.

ever become as popular as [former Boston Celtic] Larry Bird,"[67] said David Falk, Jordan's agent. Nike, a struggling athletic shoe company, paid Jordan to put his name and image on a new brand of shoes, Air Jordans. Propelled by Jordan's rising star status, Air Jordans helped Nike dominate its competition, just as Jordan dominated on the basketball court. Nike and Jordan proved that black athletes could sell products, and sell them well. Jordan became the face of Nike in the 1980s. Soon he was one of the most sought-after endorsers for everything from cereal to underwear.

In the process Jordan became a superstar. Demonstrating his universal appeal, Gatorade, a sports drink company, debuted an advertising campaign in 1991 that urged viewers to "Be Like Mike" and drink Gatorade. The catchy phrase soon became common in millions of homes across the United States. Falk said, "I don't think people look at Michael Jordan anymore and say he's a black superstar. They say he's a superstar. They totally accepted

Debi Thomas: Queen of the Ice

Figure skater Debi Thomas skated into stardom in the 1980s. In 1986 she became the first African American to win the U.S. National title. That same year Thomas won the World Figure Skating Championships and was named the Wide World of Sports Athlete of the Year.

In 1988 Thomas won the U.S. National title again and earned a spot on the Olympic team. Thomas skated strong compulsory and short programs, the first two parts of the women's figure skating competition. She led going into the final portion of the competition, the long program. However, she faltered in the long program and slipped to third place. Nevertheless, her winning the bronze medal made her the first African American to medal at the Winter Games. In 2000 Thomas was inducted into the U.S. Figure Skating Hall of Fame. When interviewed about her induction, Thomas described her feelings about being chosen by saying, "It is great to be a part of the whole skating family, and it makes me feel ecstatic that my name will be among the greats of the sport."

Quoted in ESPN.com. "Where Are They Now? Debi Thomas." February 24, 2000. http://espn.go .com/skating/news/2000/0209/345701.html.

him into the mainstream. Before he got there he might have been African American, but once he arrived, he had such a high level of acceptance that I think that the description goes away."[68]

According to basketball legend Magic Johnson, there is no question that Jordan is the greatest basketball player in history. "Michael has done things in sports, forget basketball, sports in general that no other man has done," Johnson said. "He is always going to be bigger than the game, bigger than sports. He's a world-wide hero . . . there will never be another Michael Jordan."[69]

Endorsements

Before Jordan signed his Nike deal in 1984, African American athletes had a limited presence in advertising. They appeared in some ads, usually targeting the black community. Jordan's commercial success proved that African American athletes could be very valuable as marketers to people of all races. He paved the way for other African American athletes to sign multimillion-dollar endorsement deals with major companies. "When a corporation sees Michael Jordan, they don't see race. They see him adding $200 million to sales. The color they see is green,"[70] said Brian Murphy, editor and publisher of the *Sports Marketing Letter*.

Today African American athletes are some of the highest-paid endorsers. They pitch everything from McDonald's hamburgers to cars. According to a *Sports Illustrated* report, golfer Woods ranked number one in 2010, pulling in an estimated $70 million in endorsements. Basketball star LeBron James made $30 million in 2010. "Times are changing," said Dontrell Willis, an African American Florida Marlins pitcher whom the team used in marketing campaigns during his rookie season. "We've proven we can be marketable and it's not like the past when weren't given the chance. . . . So it's not about race, it's about who can sell the best."[71]

Disappearing Public Voice

Today many African American athletes have reached the highest levels of success, influence, and power. Yet unlike earlier black stars such as heavyweight boxing champion Muhammad Ali who stood up for their beliefs, many of today's athletes are better known for their lavish lifestyles than political or social causes.

Sportswriter William C. Rhoden, author of the book *Forty Million Dollar Slaves*, has criticized modern African American athletes for their disappearing public voice on issues that matter to the black community. He wrote:

Contemporary black athletes have ridden the coattails of protest movements, benefiting from the sacrifices of the [Paul] Robesons and [Jackie] Robinsons and Jim Browns and Muhammad Alis, but have been content to be symbolic markers of progress rather than activists in their own right, pushing progress forward. They have been unwilling to collectively rock the money boat. Ironically, this new lack of interest in the larger world has occurred just at the moment in their evolution when black athletes have more economic muscle and cultural influence than ever. At a time when they could actually own the boat—rather than just rock it—the level of apathy is greater than ever before.[72]

Sportswriter William C. Rhoden has criticized modern black athletes for their disappearing public voice on issues that matter to the black community.

Room for Improvement: Coaching and Management

Although included on the playing field, African Americans' path to coaching, management, and ownership positions in sports has been slower. When Bill Russell was named player-coach of the NBA's Boston Celtics in 1966, it was the first time an African American was considered a legitimate candidate for a coaching or executive position for a major sporting team. Other pioneers followed. In 1975 the Cleveland Indians hired Frank Robinson, who became the first black manager in Major League Baseball history as manager. In 1989 Art Shell became the NFL's first African American head coach. Despite these firsts, the coaching ranks of college and professional sports have been slow to integrate African American coaches.

In the NFL, where players are predominantly African American, there are only six African American head coaches. The league has responded with efforts to increase diversity. One such effort has been dubbed the "Rooney rule," named after Dan Rooney, the owner of the Pittsburgh Steelers and chairman of the leagues diversity committee. Under the Rooney rule, NFL teams with a head coaching vacancy are required to interview at least one minority candidate for the position.

Some believe that the Rooney rule is working. They point to the hiring of coach Mike Tomlin by the Pittsburgh Steelers in 2007. At first, Tomlin, a defensive coordinator with the Minnesota Vikings, was not on the list of front-runners for the Steelers job. Said Rooney: "To be honest with you, before the interview he was just another guy who was an assistant coach. Once we interviewed him the first time, he just came through and we thought it was great. And we brought him back and talked to him on the phone and went through the process that we do, and he ended up winning the job." But Rooney also says that while the rule opened the door for Tomlin, it was the coach's credentials that got him the job. "[The rule] wasn't the most important thing because *he* was the most important thing. Mike got the job because he showed us his ability and showed us what he could do, and we believed in him,"[73] Rooney said.

Yet others believe the NFL could be doing more to promote diversity. While the Rooney rule requires teams to interview minority

Jackie Joyner-Kersee

Considered one of the best female athletes of all time, Jackie Joyner-Kersee dominated the heptathlon, a seven-event competition that consists of the 100-meter hurdles, high jump, shot put, 200 meters, 800 meters, long jump, and javelin. She was the first to score 7,000 in the event and hold the world record of 7.291 points.

Joyner-Kersee's strength, speed, and stamina won her the silver medal in the event at the 1984 Olympic Games, losing the gold by less than a second. In the 1988 and 1992 Games, she captured the gold. She also won a gold medal in 1988 and two bronzes in 1992 and 1996 for the long jump. In the opinion of Bruce Jenner, the 1976 Olympic decathlon champion, Joyner-Kersee is the greatest multi-event athlete ever.

Jackie Joyner-Kersee dominated the heptathlon in the 1980s and 1990s. She still holds the world record in the event with 7.291 points.

Under the Rooney rule, NFL teams having head-coaching vacancies are required to interview at least one minority candidate for the position. Many cite the Pittsburgh Steelers' 2007 hiring of Mike Tomlin as head coach as evidence that the rule is working.

candidates for head coaching positions, it does not impact hiring for assistant coaching positions. Studies have shown that most head coaching positions are filled through the pipeline of assistant coaches. At the start of the 2009 season, only twelve minorities held one of the league's sixty-seven coordinator positions. John Solow, an economics professor in the University of Iowa's Tippie College of Business, who cowrote a paper on the impact of the Rooney rule on minority hiring in the NFL, said:

> If the league introduced African-American coaches into the front of the pipeline instead of at the end, more of those coaches would have the experience teams are looking for and be more likely to be hired as head coaches. By encouraging minorities to think earlier in their careers to consider coaching when their collegiate playing careers end, the NFL could

increase the number of minority assistant coaches generally and ultimately, their representation among head coaches.[74]

Yet there are signs of progress. The 2010–2011 college football season had thirteen African American men leading football programs, more than any year in history. "You have to think about all of the African-American coaches that came before you and you guys now have a chance to make history and do something those guys never had a chance to do," said Charlie Strong, head football coach at the University of Louisville. "It's just small steps that we're taking, but we know that those steps will take us somewhere."[75]

In addition, the NBA has become a leader in coaching diversity. According to a 2010 study, eight African American head coaches led teams in the 2009 season. In addition, 41 percent of assistant coaches were people of color. In the front offices, the NBA was the leader in men's professional sports for having more African American team presidents and other senior administrative officials in clubs' front offices.

Ownership

On December 17, 2002, Robert Johnson became the principal owner of the NBA's Charlotte Bobcats. He was the first black majority owner of a professional sports franchise in the modern era. Other black businesspeople had owned sports teams, but they were black teams in black leagues. Johnson crossed the color line of ownership. "After a while, the race issue dissipates for most people," he said after buying the Bobcats. "At the end of the day, what's going to make the difference in this business or any other business is: Can you put a product out there that people want to be involved in? If you do that, nobody's going to care what color the owner is. Nobody's going to care much about the owner at all."[76]

Few African American businesspeople have joined Johnson in ownership of professional sporting teams. In 2010 Jordan bought out Johnson as the owner of the Bobcats. While some African Americans hold minority interests in sports teams, as of 2011 Jordan remains the only African American majority owner in men's pro sports. No African Americans are majority owners in Major League Baseball. No person of color has ever held a majority ownership interest in an NFL team.

African Americans and Hockey

In 1958 Canadian-born Willie O'Ree became the National Hockey League's (NHL's) first black player when he entered a game as a left winger for the Boston Bruins. He played two games with the Bruins, then was sent down to the minors for two more. He did not come back into the NHL until 1961, when he played forty-three games. No other black athlete played in the NHL until 1974, when the Washington Capitals drafted Mike Marson.

Since then, hockey has not had many black players. Those who do play are frequently Canadian. The expense of youth hockey and competition of players from Russia and Europe for NHL roster spots have limited the opportunities for African American athletes. To address the issue, the NHL has a Diversity Task Force, a nonprofit program designed to introduce children of diverse ethnic backgrounds to hockey. They have also developed the Used Equipment Bank, which encourages people to donate their used equipment to economically disadvantaged youth hockey players.

From jockey Isaac Murphy to golfer Woods, African American athletes have made headlines for more than a century. Their path to fame and fortune has not always been easy. They were pioneers in many sports and laid the foundation for those who came after. If not for tennis star Gibson and golfer Charlie Sifford, stars like the Williams sisters and Woods may not have been able to achieve the success that they have today. With each success and milestone, these men and women served as symbols of hope, pride, and unity for the African American community.

The journey of the black athlete has also been a reflection of the journey of the African American community. Some athletes chose to use their spotlight to call for social and legal changes. By doing so, these men and women risked their personal careers in order to stand up for what they believed was right. "I believe that's the true measure of greatness in sports—when the actions of athletes transcend the playing field and affect the way we live,"[77] wrote Tony Dungy, former head coach of the NFL Indianapolis Colts and the first African American head coach to win the Super Bowl.

Notes

Introduction: African American Trailblazers

1. Quoted in ESPN.com. "Dungy Becomes First Black Coach to Win Super Bowl." February 4, 2007. http://sports.espn.go.com/nfl/play offs06/news/story?id=2754521.
2. Quoted in Warren Richey. "A Super Bowl First: Two Black Head Coaches." *Christian Science Monitor*, February 2, 2007. www.cs monitor.com/2007/0202/p01s03-ussc.html.
3. Quoted in Susan Reed. "Arthur Ashe Remembers the Forgotten Men of Sport—America's Early Black Athletes." *People.com*, March 6, 1989. www.people.com/people/archive/article/0,,20119720,00.html.
4. Quoted in Peter Kelley. "Stories of Strength Shine in 'Better than the Best: Black Athletes Speak, 1920–2007.'" *UW Today*, February 9, 2011. www.washington.edu/news/articles/stories-of-strength-shine-in-walter2019s-2018better-than-the-best-black-athletes-speak-1920-20072019.

Chapter One: African Americans in Nineteenth-Century Sports

5. Quoted in William C. Rhoden. *Forty Million Dollar Slaves: The Rise, Fall, and Redemption of the Black Athlete*. New York: Random House, 2006, p. 52.
6. Quoted in Russell T. Wigginton. *The Strange Career of the Black Athlete*. Westport, CT: Praeger, 2006, p. 6.
7. Quoted in Rhoden. *Forty Million Dollar Slaves*, p. 76.
8. Quoted in Lynne Tolman. "'Worcester Whirlwind' Overcame Bias." *Telegram & Gazette*, July 23, 1995. www.majortaylorassociation.org/whirlwind.htm.
9. Quoted in Rhoden. *Forty Million Dollar Slaves*, p. 81.

Chapter Two: Playing in Separate Leagues

10. Booker T. Washington. "1895 Atlanta Compromise Speech." History Matters. http://historymatters.gmu.edu/d/39.
11. Quoted in Robert Peterson. *Only the Ball Was White: A History of Legendary Black Players and All-Black Professional Teams*. New York: Gramercy, 1970, p. 65.
12. Quoted in Peterson. *Only the Ball Was White*, p. 83.
13. Quoted in Peterson. *Only the Ball Was White*, p. 160.
14. Quoted in Larry Schwartz. "No Joshing About Gibson's Talents."

ESPN.com. http://espn.go.com/sportscentury/features/00016050.html.

15. Quoted in Peterson. *Only the Ball Was White*, p. 133.

16. Quoted in M.B. Roberts. "Paige Never Looked Back." ESPN.com. http://espn.go.com/sportscentury/features/00016396.html.

17. Quoted in Roberts. "Paige Never Looked Back."

18. Quoted in John Hareas. "Remembering the Rens." NBA.com. www.nba.com/history/encyclopedia_rens_001214.html.

19. Quoted in Hareas. "Remembering the Rens."

20. Quoted in Hareas. "Remembering the Rens."

21. Quoted in *Unforgivable Blackness: The Rise and Fall of Jack Johnson*. "About the Film." PBS.org. www.pbs.org/unforgivableblackness/about.

22. Quoted in *The Fight*. "Jack Johnson." PBS.org, September 22, 2004. www.pbs.org/wgbh/amex/fight/peopleevents/p_johnson.html.

23. Quoted in *Unforgivable Blackness: The Rise and Fall of Jack Johnson*. "About the Film."

24. Quoted in Larry Schwartz. "Brown Bomber Was a Hero to All." ESPN.com. http://espn.go.com/sportscentury/features/00016109.html.

25. Quoted in Schwartz. "Brown Bomber Was a Hero to All."

26. Quoted in *The Fight*. "Joe Louis." PBS.org, September 22, 2004. www.pbs.org/wgbh/amex/fight/peopleevents/p_louis.html.

27. Quoted in Larry Schwartz. "Owens Pierced a Myth." ESPN.com. http://espn.go.com/sportscentury/features/00016393.html.

28. Quoted in Schwartz. "Owens Pierced a Myth."

29. Quoted in JesseOwens.com. "Jesse Owens: Olympic Legend." www.jesseowens.com/about.

Chapter Three: Breaking the Color Line

30. Quoted in Andrew Schall. "The Next Page/Wendell Smith: The Pittsburgh Journalist Who Made Jackie Robinson Mainstream." *Pittsburgh Post Gazette*, June 5, 2011. www.post-gazette.com/pg/11156/1151192-109-0.stm#ixzz1Ot5FtMka.

31. Quoted in David K. Wiggins. *Glory Bound: Black Athletes in a White America*. Syracuse: Syracuse University Press, 1997, p. 91.

32. Quoted in Wiggins. *Glory Bound*, p. 101.

33. Quoted in Wiggins. *Glory Bound*, p. 101.

34. Quoted in Wiggins. *Glory Bound*, p. 102.

35. Quoted in Jerome Holtzman. "How Wendell Smith Helped Robinson's Cause." *Chicago*

Tribune, March 31, 1997. http://articles.chicagotribune.com/1997-03-31/sports/9703310169_1_clyde-sukeforth-jackie-robinson-kansas-city-monarchs.

36. Quoted in Peterson, *Only the Ball Was White*, p. 190.

37. Quoted in Larry Schwartz. "Jackie Changed Face of Sports." ESPN.com. http://espn.go.com/sportscentury/features/00016431.html.

38. Quoted in Schwartz. "Jackie Changed Face of Sports."

39. John C. Walter. "The Changing Status of the Black Athlete in the 20th Century United States." *American Studies Today*, Summer 1996. www.americansc.org.uk/Online/walters.htm.

Chapter Four: An Uneven Progress

40. Quoted in Jim Gullo. "A Salute to Sweet Swinger." *Sports Illustrated*, May 31, 1993. http://sportsillustrated.cnn.com/vault/article/magazine/MAG1138243/1/index.htm.

41. Quoted in Gullo. "A Salute to Sweet Swinger."

42. Quoted in PGA Village. "PGA Museum of Golf Unveils African-American Exhibit." www.pgavillage.com/stlucie/index.cfm?page=african_american_golf_pioneers.

43. Quoted in American Tennis Association. "History—the Black Tennis Mecca." www.american

tennisassociation.org/aboutus/history.php.

44. Quoted in *Time*. "Sport: That Gibson Girl." August 26, 1957. www.time.com/time/magazine/article/0,9171,862710,00.html#ixzz1PBe25vuw.

45. Quoted in Larry Schwartz. "Althea Gibson Broke Barriers." ESPN.com. http://espn.go.com/sportscentury/features/00014035.html.

46. Quoted in Roxanne Jones, Jessie Paolucci, and Tony Dungy. *Say It Loud: An Illustrated History of the Black Athlete*. New York: Balantine, 2010, p. 165.

47. Quoted in Schwartz. "Althea Gibson Broke Barriers."

48. Quoted in Jones et al. *Say It Loud*, p. 166.

49. Quoted in ATP World Tour. "Arthur Ashe." www.atpworldtour.com/Tennis/Players/As/A/Arthur-R-Ashe.aspx.

Chapter Five: The Civil Rights Era: Athletes Speak for Change

50. Quoted in George Vecsey. "Indomitable Russell Values One Accolade Above the Rest." *New York Times*, February 12, 2011. www.nytimes.com/2011/02/13/sports/basketball/13russell.html?pagewanted=2&_r=2.

51. Quoted in Sean Deveney. "Bill Russell's 11 Championships." *Sporting News*, April 25, 2011.

52. Quoted in Jones et al. *Say It Loud*, p. 76.

53. Quoted in Vecsey. "Indomitable Russell Values One Accolade Above the Rest."

54. Quoted in Russell T. Wigginton. *The Strange Career of the Black Athlete*. Westport, CT: Praeger, 2006, p. 52.

55. Quoted in Wigginton, *The Strange Career of the Black Athlete*, p. 57.

56. Quoted in Steve Rushin. "Jim Brown." *Sports Illustrated*, November 21, 2007. http://sportsillus trated.cnn.com/vault/article/magazine/MAG1115837/index.htm.

57. Quoted in Rushin. "Jim Brown."

58. Quoted in Alex Poinsett. "The Controversial Jim Brown." *Ebony*, December 1964, p. 65.

59. Quoted in Wigginton. *The Strange Career of the Black Athlete*, p. 63.

60. Quoted in Jesse Abramson. "Cassius Clay Scores 'Incredible' Title Fight Triumph." *Ottawa Citizen*, February 28, 1964. http://news .google.com/newspapers?id=ZbM yAAAAIBAJ&sjid=i-wFAAAAIBAJ &pg=4391,2972708&dq=cassius +clay+defeats+liston&hl=en.

61. Quoted in Robert Lipsyte. "Clay Refuses Army Oath; Stripped of Boxing Crown." *New York Times*, April 29, 1967. www.nytimes .com/books/98/10/25/specials/ ali-army.html.

62. Quoted in David Davis. "Taking a Stand." *Smithsonian*, August 2008, p. 12.

63. Quoted in Amy Bass. *Not the Triumph but the Struggle: The 1968 Olympics and the Making of the Black Athlete*. Minneapolis: University of Minnesota Press, 2002, p. 271.

Chapter Six: Rising to the Top

64. Ed Berliner. "Tiger Woods: The Greatest Athlete of This Generation." Bleacher Report, March 30, 2009. http://bleacherreport .com/articles/147750-tiger-woods-the-greatest-athlete-of-this-generation.

65. Quoted in ESPN.com. "Venus, Serena Playing Night of Tribute to Althea Gibson." August 27, 2007. http://sports.espn.go.com/sports/ tennis/usopen07/news/story?id=2 988000.

66. Quoted in Clare Martin. "Jordan's Three Act Play in the NBA." NBA.com. www.nba.com/jordan/ clareonjordan.html.

67. Quoted in Rhoden. *Forty Million Dollar Slaves*, p. 203.

68. Quoted in Rhoden. *Forty Million Dollar Slaves*, p. 204.

69. Quoted in David DuPree. "Jordan Wears 'Greatest' Crown." *USA Today*, February 6, 2003. www.usatoday.com/sports/basket ball/nba/2003-02-06-dupree-team_x.htm.

70. Quoted in Jon Morgan. "Black Sports Stars Dominate Ads Endorsements." *Baltimore Sun*, February 27, 1998. http://articles .baltimoresun.com/1998-02-27/news/1998058039_1_black-

athletes-calvin-hill-michael-jordan.

71. Quoted in Darren Rovell. "The Technicolor Sports Hero." ESPN.com, February 27, 2004. http://sports.espn.go.com/espn/blackhistory/news/story?id=1745914.

72. Rhoden. *Forty Million Dollar Slaves*, p. 217.

73. Quoted in Greg Garber. "Thanks to Rooney Rule, Doors Opened." ESPN.com, February 9, 2007. http://sports.espn.go.com/nfl/playoffs06/news/story?id=2750645.

74. Quoted in University of Iowa. "Study Finds NFL's Rooney Rule Does Little to Help Minority Head Coaching Hiring." January 12, 2010. http://news-releases .uiowa.edu/2010/january/\011210blackNFLcoach.html.

75. Quoted in Eric King. "Black Coaches Have Big Dreams for Football." WLKY.com, February 20, 2010. www.wlky.com/r/22636226/detail.html.

76. Quoted in *Jet*. "BET Founder Bob Johnson First Black Majority Owner of Sports Franchise." *Jet*, January 13, 2003, p. 48.

77. Quoted in Jones et al. *Say It Loud*, p. vii.

For More Information

Books

Nathan Aaseng. *African-American Athletes (A to Z of African Americans)*. New York: Facts On File, 2011. This book profiles more than 155 athletes, with information on their lives and their athletic accomplishments.

Jim Gigliotti. *Jesse Owens: Gold Medal Hero*. New York: Sterling, 2010. This book profiles track star Jesse Owens and his sprint to gold in the 1936 Berlin Olympic Games.

Cecil Harris and Larryette Kyle-DeBose. *Charging the Net: A History of Blacks in Tennis from Althea Gibson and Arthur Ashe to the Williams Sisters*. Chicago: Ivan R. Dee, 2007. This book follows black tennis through the twentieth and early twenty-first centuries.

Roxanne Jones, Jessie Paolucci, and Tony Dungy. *Say It Loud: An Illustrated History of the Black Athlete*. New York: ESPN, 2010. This book profiles African American athletes whose accomplishments changed the game and transcended the playing field.

Kadir Nelson. *We Are the Ship: The Story of Negro League Baseball*. New York: Hyperion, 2008. The book tells the story of the Negro leagues from the point of view of an unnamed narrator, telling tales of the great players who forged the path toward breaking the race barrier.

Charles E. Pedersen. *Jackie Robinson: Baseball Great & Civil Rights Activist*. Edina, MN: ABDO, 2009. This book profiles baseball player Jackie Robinson and his journey into Major League Baseball.

Stephen Timblin. *Muhammad Ali: King of the Ring*. New York: Sterling, 2010. This book offers a succinct account of controversial boxer Muhammad Ali's life.

Russell T. Wigginton. *The Strange Career of the Black Athlete: African Americans and Sport*. Westport, CT: Praeger, 2006. This book presents a review of the sometimes tumultuous rise of black athletes in the United States. It explores the role of black athletes in predominantly white sports and the role of black athletes in the civil rights era and beyond.

Websites

African American Athletes (www.bio graphy.com/blackhistory/people/at hletes.jsp). This website features links to biographies of famous African American athletes.

History of Jim Crow (www.jimcrow history.org). This website offers essays and details about historical events in the struggle for black freedom and rights.

Jackie Robinson (www.jackierobinson .com). The official website of Jackie Robinson contains stats, photos, and a biography of Robinson's life.

National Baseball Hall of Fame (http://baseballhall.org). This website features biographies, stats, and a transcript of the induction speech for each member of the Hall of Fame.

Negro League Baseball (www.negro leaguebaseball.com). This website has a Negro league timeline and information about the Negro league teams and individual players.

Negro Leagues Baseball Museum (www.nlbm.com). This website has information about the history of the Negro leagues as well as a link to an e-museum with player and team profiles.

Top North American Athletes of the Century (http://espn.go.com/ sportscentury/athletes.html). This website presents articles about the greatest athletes of the twentieth century, profiled by ESPN as part of the SportsCentury retrospective.

Index

Picture Credits

Cover: © Bettmann/Corbis
AP Images, 24, 62, 82
AP Images/Bill Waugh, 88
AP Images/Carolyn Kaster, 74
AP Images/Chuck Burton, 97
AP Images/Michael Conroy, 10
AP Images/Pro Football Hall of Fame/NFL, 53
Augusta National/Getty Images, 58
© Bettmann/Corbis, 25, 37, 44, 57, 61, 70
Bob Gomel/Time & Life Pictures/Getty Images, 65
Bud Skinner/MCT/Landov, 84
Central Press/Getty Images, 41, 79
Chicago History Museum/Getty Images, 19
Curt Gunther/Keystone/Archive Photos/Getty Images, 48
Diamond Images/Getty Images, 29
Edward Gooch/Getty Images, 20
GLYN KIRK/AFP/Getty Images, 89
IOC/Allsport/Getty Images, 67
Joe Robbins/Getty Images, 94
© Laszlo Szirtesi/Alamy, 51
Mark Rucker/Transcendental Graphics/Getty Images, 33, 34
New York Daily News Archive via Getty Images, 39
© North Wind Picture Archives/Alamy, 14
Photo File/MLB Photos via Getty Images, 81
Popperphoto/Getty Images, 23
Rogers Photo Archive/Getty Images, 49
Scott Olson/Reuters/Landov, 91
Tony Duffy/Allsport/Getty Images, 96
Tony Tomsic/Getty Images, 76
Transcendental Graphics/Getty Images, 28

About the Author

Carla Mooney is the author of several books and articles for young readers. She loves investigating and learning about little-known people, places, and events in our history. A graduate of the University of Pennsylvania, she lives in Pittsburgh with her husband and three children.